Creating Effective
Enrollment Management
Systems

Creating Effective Enrollment Management Systems

Don Hossler

New York, College Entrance Examination Board, 1986

For our boys,
David, Peter, and Jonathan

Copies of this book may be ordered from College Board Publications, Box 866, New York, New York 10101. The price is $12.95.

Editorial inquiries concerning this book should be addressed to: Editorial Office, The College Board, 45 Columbus Avenue, New York, New York 10023-6917.

Library of Congress Catalog Number: 86-071538

ISBN: 0-87447-272-5

Printed in the United States of America

9 8 7 6 5 4 3 2 1

Contents

Preface

Although the term "enrollment management" may be new, the concept is not. It has been in the process of development for several years. In fact, if we examine the evolution of the offices of admissions and financial aid along with other areas of student affairs, and follow the emergence of marketing in higher education, and research on student college choice and student persistence, it becomes evident that the enrollment management paradigm represents the convergence of developments in each of these areas.

It would be difficult to unravel these developments so as to determine whether the competitive nature of college admissions in the last 20 years has caused the advances made in the field of nonprofit marketing for higher education or whether the emergence of nonprofit marketing has made possible the increasing sophistication of college recruitment activities. It would be equally difficult to ascertain whether our increasingly differentiated financial aid and pricing activities are solely the product of greater competition for students or whether research on student college choice and the effects of aid and price on college choice have resulted in more effective aid and pricing policies. With respect to student attrition, student impact studies and student fit research have produced institutional retention programs that are increasingly tailored to meet the needs of student populations at specific institutions. The point to be made is that emergence of the enrollment management paradigm should not be viewed as a "new" approach to influencing student enrollments. Rather, it should be seen as part of an ongoing process that has enabled college and university administrators to exert greater influence over the factors that shape their institutions' enrollments.

Viewed from this evolutionary perspective it is not surprising that some college administrators have not been impressed with this "new" concept of enrollment management. A few campuses have been engaged in some form of enrollment management activities for several years. Many selective colleges and universities have traditionally given careful attention to characteristics of their entering classes. The Consortium on the Financing of Higher Education (COFHE) institutions, comprised of most of the Ivy League colleges plus institutions such as Stanford and Carleton, have been engaged in cooperative studies of marketing, student college choice, and financial aid policies for many years. The works of Huddleston (1984) and Ihlanfeldt (1980) suggest that Bradley University and Northwestern University were engaged in enrollment management practices before that concept had been formally articulated and described. These early enrollment management efforts had some of the following characteristics:

1. Continual analysis of the institution's image in the student marketplace.
2. Attention to the connections between recruitment and financial aid policies.
3. An early willingness to adopt sound marketing principles in recruitment activities.
4. A recognition of the importance of gathering and utilizing information to guide institutional practices and policies.

As is often the case, writings that have described these emerging systems approaches to college enrollments lagged behind the actual development of the systems. Scholars and educational observers frequently find themselves in the position of following institutional trends by describing emerging developments, thus formalizing them. One of the first times the term enrollment management formally appears is in a 1981 *College Board Review* article by Kreutner and Godfrey. Their article describes a matrix approach to managing enrollments developed at California State University at Long Beach. This was followed by Maguire and Lay's (1980; 1981) articles describing enrollment management efforts at Boston College; *Strategies for Effective Enrollment Management* by Kemerer, Baldridge, and Green (1982); and *Enrollment Management: An Integrated Approach* by Hossler (1984). This formalizing process appears to have lent legitimacy to these new ways of influencing enrollments and has been at least partially responsible for the increased interest in the concept of enrollment management.

This book continues this process of formalizing the enrollment management concept. It is written primarily for three audiences: those administrators who currently engage in an enrollment management system; those who are in the process of developing an enrollment management system; and those who are interested in gaining exposure to the concept. The third group should also read earlier works such as *Strategies for Effective Enrollment Management* (1982) by Kemerer, Baldridge, and Green and *Enrollment Management: An Integrated Approach* (1984) by Hossler.

Chapters 1 through 3 attempt to add to our understanding of the elements of an enrollment management system. Chapter 1 begins with a description of the current issues that are shaping traditional student enrollments. It then moves on to define and outline the concept of enrollment management and to introduce the basic elements of an enrollment management system. In addition, this chapter examines the enrollment management concept from broader organizational perspectives such as management systems and management science. Such perspectives assist campus-based administrators who wish to adapt existing models to fit the specific contexts of their institutions.

Chapter 2 examines in greater detail the elements and their relationships in an idealized enrollment management system. It also presents a review of the organizational models for managing enrollments that were developed by Kemerer, Baldridge, and Green (1982) and discusses them from a tightly coupled systems perspective. The purpose of this chapter is to provide examples of how enrollment management administrative structures and activities can be based on market research, student impact research, and organizational theory. The examples of these principles are not exhaustive but are illustrative of potential applications.

Chapter 3 looks at the issue of establishing an enrollment management system. More specifically, it explores a variety of approaches to organizational change that demonstrate that change is determined more by organizational and environmental factors than by the change strategies employed. This requires enrollment managers to be good organizational and environmental diagnosticians if they want to implement an enrollment management system.

Following the first three chapters, four case studies are presented. These case studies are written by administrators at public and private, two- and four-year institutions. These individuals have played an integral role in the development of an enrollment management model on their respective campuses. These chapters provide insights into how different enrollment management systems can be implemented, as well as reveal some of the unique characteristics of systems that have emerged to fit the needs of different institutions. The case studies, when considered in the context of the first three chapters, provide enrollment managers with a range of ideas that can be used to develop an effective enrollment management system.

Acknowledgments

The seeds for this book came from countless discussions with admissions officers, financial aid personnel, student affairs administrators, and faculty members, in addition to a number of people at The College Board who have an interest in the concept of enrollment management. My initial interest in this area was in the relationship between a range of research issues and their applications to college enrollments. However, I found that my discussions of the utility of research for those interested in influencing college enrollments frequently led to organizational and programmatic questions. This book is an attempt to address many of these questions.

A number of people have been helpful in conceptualizing and completing this project. Extensive conversations on the topic of enrollment management with Steve Graff, Darrell Morris, and Terry Novak of The College Board, and with David Weiss at the Educational Testing Service have been particularly helpful in making sense out of many of the issues that are addressed in this book. In addition, the thoughts of Frank Kemerer at North Texas State University, Larry Litten at the Consortium on the Financing of Higher Education, David Davis-Van Atta at Oberlin College, and David Clark and George Kuh at Indiana University have helped me to tease out some of the programmatic and organizational ideas that I have used here.

It is much easier to "think" about the ideas that "could" be a book than it is to refine them to the point where they become clear enough to be put into print. I would like to thank Sue Buffington, my graduate assistant, and Steve Graff at the Midwestern Regional Office of The College Board, along with Darrell Morris and Jim Nelson at the New York Office of The College Board, for their editorial suggestions. I also want to acknowledge Sarah Cochran, the office secretary, who did everything from typing to making tables. Most important, I want to thank my wife Carol-Anne and our three children, David, Peter, and Jonathan, for their support and understanding over the past year.

Chapter 1

Defining Enrollment Management: A Tightly Coupled System

THE CURRENT CONTEXT

College enrollments have been projected to fall significantly by the 1990s in some regions of the United States (Crossland 1980). Frances (1984) reports a total decline of 40 percent in the number of 18- to 21-year-olds between 1979 and 1994 (p. 4). Thus far, however, the steep projected declines have failed to materialize. In 1984 total college enrollments remained stable (*Chronicle of Higher Education,* December 12, 1984, p. 1, hereafter cited as *Chronicle*). In 1985, total enrollments fell by less than 1 percent (*Chronicle,* October 30, 1985, p. 1). In fact, the 1980s has not been an era of significant enrollment declines as predicted. Rather, enrollments have stabilized with years of small decreases or increases (*Chronicle,* November 24, 1982, p. 7; October 27, 1983, p. 14; and October 30, 1985, p. 1).

Up until now, colleges and universities have been successful, and may continue to be successful, in maintaining student enrollments in spite of the decline in the number of traditional-age college students. A number of demographic and public policy shifts are converging, however, which will have an effect on student enrollments.

Demographic shifts as well as public policy trends at the state and federal level are affecting financial aid, high school graduation standards, and college entrance requirements. This first category of developments is likely to have a negative impact on the supply of college matriculants. In addition, a second category of state initiatives is influencing the internal policies of many public institutions, thus affecting the ability of these colleges and universities to attract students. Increasing state interest in coordinating academic programs to avoid duplication and to ensure quality, along with attempts to monitor student outcomes, is affecting public colleges and universities. The impact of these initiatives on student enrollments may be both positive and negative.

Demographic Trends

Most higher education policy makers have failed to recognize that the realities of traditional-age student enrollments may be even bleaker than the projections. Until recently, demographic projections for high school graduation rates have used aggregate data. Aggregate figures mask the changing make-up of our population. The numbers of minorities, particularly Asian, black, and Hispanic students, as well as their proportional representation among the school-age population, are increasing steadily (Hodgkinson 1983). As Hodgkinson has pointed out, the changing nature of the high school population has important implications for American higher education. In some states, the majority white student is rapidly becoming the minority student. This change in the ethnic and racial make-up of current elementary and secondary students will have an impact on colleges and universities in ways that go beyond simple demographics. In fact, three trends are converging that could reduce college enrollments by more than the current predictions, which are based only on demographics.

As Table 1.1 illustrates, institutions of higher education may see a major shift in the racial and ethnic composition of their student bodies. The increase in the number of Hispanic and Asian students is striking. In states like California and Texas, Hispanics represented over 40 percent of all students enrolled in public schools in 1980 (Hodgkinson 1983, p. 6). By the year 2000, over half of all youths in California will be minorities (p. 5). A recent report from the National Center for Educational Statistics reveals that there are only 14 states in the United States in which minority public school enrollments are less than 10 percent (Hodgkinson 1985, p. 4). In 18 states, the percentage of minority enrollments exceeds 35 percent. Without this increase in the number of minority students, the decline in the traditional-age student cohort would be 24 percent greater than it is already expected to be (Hodgkinson 1983, p. 7). Despite the increase in certain racial and ethnic groups, however, when all student groups in total are considered, high school graduation rates will continue to decline until 1992 (*Chronicle* 1985, pp. 1, 18). This decline, however, may be further accentuated by other factors that will also be examined in this section.

Despite the gloomy projected declines in total college enrollments, shortfalls have failed to materialize in the magnitude predicted by many policy analysts. The reason most often cited for stable enrollments is the increase in the number of adult students who have entered institutions of higher education. Between 1972 and 1983 the percentage of women over

Table 1.1. Minority Public School Enrollment, Fall 1980

State and Region	Percentage of Total Enrollment	State and Region	Percentage of Total Enrollment
United States	26.7	Southeast	
		Alabama	33.6
New England		Arkansas	23.5
Connecticut	17.0	Florida	32.2
Maine	0.9	Georgia	34.3
Massachusetts	10.7	Kentucky	9.1
New Hampshire	1.3	Louisiana	43.4
Rhode Island	8.2	Mississippi	51.6
Vermont	1.0	North Carolina	31.9
		South Carolina	43.5
Mideast		Tennessee	24.5
Delaware	28.8	Virginia	27.5
District of Columbia	96.4	West Virginia	4.3
Maryland	33.5		
New Jersey	28.4	Southwest	
New York	32.0	Arizona	33.7
Pennsylvania	14.9	New Mexico	57.0
		Oklahoma	20.8
Great Lakes		Texas	45.9
Illinois	28.6		
Indiana	12.0	Rocky Mountain	
Michigan	21.3	Colorado	22.1
Ohio	14.7	Idaho	8.2
Wisconsin	9.3	Montana	12.1
		Utah	7.3
Plains		Wyoming	7.5
Iowa	4.1		
Kansas	12.7	Far West	
Minnesota	5.9	California	42.9
Missouri	14.8	Nevada	18.9
Nebraska	10.5	Oregon	8.5
North Dakota	3.5	Washington	14.1
South Dakota	7.9	Alaska	28.4
		Hawaii	75.2

From Hodgkinson 1983. These data were presented at a conference sponsored by the Institute for Educational Leadership on November 17, 1982.

the age of 24 enrolled in higher education rose by 13 percent. The numer of males in the same age group rose by only 4 percent (*Statistical Abstracts of the United States* 1985). Between 1980 and 1983, however, the percentage of women in this age group has risen by only 3 percent and the percentage of men by only 1 percent (p. 148). Current projections from the National Center of Educational Statistics estimate only a 4 percent increase between 1987 and 1992 in the number of students 25 years or older who will attend a college or university (U.S. Department of Education

1985). Frances (1984) states that the adult student population has peaked and can no longer be counted on as a source of new students. Just as the number of traditional-age students is about to begin one of its steepest declines, it appears that an increase in adult students is unlikely to offset this decline.

Effects of Public Policy on the Supply of College Matriculants

Demographic trends alone should no longer be considered the only impetus for interest among institutions for greater control over their student enrollments. Recent shifts in social values and attitudes and an accompanying change in public policies have also had an impact on college student enrollments. The current concern over the quality of education has brought a great deal of attention to the quality of high school preparation. Growing competition for federal and state dollars (which is likely to be accentuated by the Gramm-Rudman-Hollings bill) has resulted in changing student financial aid policies, which have had an effect on student enrollments.

As the public debate over the quality of American education has intensified, a number of states have enacted legislation to improve the quality of education (Hodgkinson 1985). At the high school level this has resulted in the strengthening of graduation requirements, competency testing prior to graduation, and a number of other measures designed to induce more rigor into secondary schooling. The companion report to *A Nation at Risk* (1983), *The Nation Responds* (1984), reports that 48 states have changed or are reviewing their high school graduation requirements and that 19 states have put into place or are considering developing new placement tests or promotion examinations (p. 78). A recent American Council on Education (ACE) survey (El-Khawas 1985) found that 47 percent of all colleges were either reviewing or had recently completed a review of their admission requirements. This has led to requiring entering high school graduates to take more mathematics, science, English, and foreign language courses before coming to an institution of higher education.

The long-term effects of the emphasis on educational quality are difficult to determine. Green (1982) believes that in the long run this policy shift will produce a greater number of better prepared high school graduates, which will increase the number of graduates going on to college. In addition he believes that retention rates will improve because these future college students will require less remediation and be more likely to experience academic success. However, predicting the future is always difficult.

An alternative scenario is that the educational excellence movement will result in fewer high school graduates. For instance, a Southern Regional Board of Education report (*Chronicle,* January 8, 1986, pp. 1, 9) predicts that, unless the academic preparation of students improves, there will be a decline in the number of black high school students who go on to college. This will be the product of rising expectations for high school students without accompanying academic support systems. As a result more students will become discouraged and drop out of high school, or they will be unable to pass competency tests so that they can graduate. In Florida, where competency tests have been required of all high school seniors, 100,000 seniors did not pass the competency examination in 1984 and were unable to receive their high school diplomas. Mikulecky's studies of the National Assessment of Educational Progress (1985) have shown that only 4.9 percent of all high school graduates could perform tasks at the advanced level (p. 3).[1] When analyzing the academic skills of entering college freshmen he concludes that (p. 3):

- A typical open admissions college could expect less than 10 percent to be able to read at the advanced level and as many as 16 percent to be reading at the intermediate level (the intermediate reading level is the reading level of the average 13-year-old).
- A selective college (drawing from the top quarter of all high school graduates) can expect 20 percent to be able to read at the advanced level.

If the events in Florida represent one of the outcomes of the excellence movement, even fewer high school graduates can be anticipated.

Along with policy shifts that are intended to influence the quality of education in the United States, trends in the financing of higher education also appear to be having an impact on college enrollments. Shifting budgetary priorities and growing concern over the federal deficit have had an impact on student financial aid. Gillespie and Carlson (1985, p. 1) document a steady decline in the real dollar value of financial aid. Between

1. The reading levels used to analyze the results reported in Mikulecky's study include:

   a. Rudimentary: . . . Can select words or phrases to describe a simple picture . . . The ability to carry out simple, discrete reading tasks.

   b. Basic: . . . Has learned basic comprehenson strategies . . . the ability to understand specific or sequentially related information.

   c. Intermediate: . . . Can make inferences and reach generalizations . . . the ability to search for specific information, interrelate ideas, and make generalizations.

   d. Adept: . . . Can understand complicated literary passages and integrate informal material . . . the ability to find, understand, summarize, and explain relatively complicated information.

   e. Advanced: . . . Can extend and restructure ideas . . . understand the links between ideas . . . the ability to synthesize and learn from specialized material.

1963 and 1967 the value of student financial aid increased ten-fold. Since 1981 the real dollar value of student financial aid has declined by 21 percent. Along with the declining value of financial aid awards there is a growing trend to award financial aid on the basis of merit as well as need (Haines 1984). While some aid observers have argued that this need not detract from society's commitments to access and equity, others have asserted that financial aid is a "fixed pie" and that merit awards by necessity reduce the amount of aid available for need-based awards.

Further exacerbating the impact of the declining value of financial aid has been a constant drift toward a "market approach" to tuition in the public sector (Hearn and Loganecker 1985). Public institutions have increasingly come to rely on tuition increases as opposed to direct public subsidies to fund institutional budgets. The philosophy behind the market model posits that reductions of public subsidies to high-income students and greater use of financial aid as a means to aid low-income students produces a more efficient use of public funds without reducing access or equity. This approach, however, results in increased demand for financial aid funds during a time of great pressure to hold steady or decrease the amount of state and federal dollars that are allocated for financial aid. Rising tuition costs coupled with reductions in the value of financial aid typically reduce the numbers of low-income students who will pursue higher education. Low-income students are the most sensitive to increases in the cost of attending college (Manski and Wise 1983) and may become increasingly discouraged as tuition costs rise.

Most recently, the passage of the Gramm-Rudman-Hollings bill (Balanced Budget and Emergency Deficit Control Act of 1985) will add to the problem of the diminishing value of financial aid by producing a decline in the current dollar value of financial aid. A recent report from the Washington Office of The College Board (*Update,* January 1986, p. 6) estimates that if Gramm-Rudman goes into effect, the total amount allocated to Pell Grants is likely to fall to 2.6 billion dollars by 1986–87. Campus-based aid programs (College Work Study, National Direct Student Loan, and Supplemental Educational Opportunity Grant) will fall to 1.4 billion dollars by 1986–87. In constant dollars this is less than was allocated for Pell Grants at any time in the past seven years. For campus-based aid programs, this drops the level of allocations in current dollars to pre-1980 levels.

Reductions in federal aid programs are likely to continue this shift toward a market approach to tuition costs. This is evident from the effects of Gramm-Rudman on loan programs. For the Guaranteed Student Loan (GSL) program the loan origination fee paid by borrowers is increased and the special allowance payment to lenders during the first year of the loan is reduced. Both moves place the GSL program more in line with the realities of money markets and the cost of borrowing in the banking industry at large. The effect of the Gramm-Rudman-Hollings bill on federal financial aid may result in a reduction in the enrollment rates of traditional-age college students. At best it may produce a shift from private to public institutions; at worst it may reduce total aggregate enrollments. Minority and low-income students may be particularly hard-hit by this legislation.

A Profile of Future Matriculants

Future college enrollments are certain to be comprised of more minority students. Unless there is a large redistribution of income in the near future, many of these high school students are likely to be low-income students. Hodgkinson's data show that 48 percent of all children born in 1980 will be raised in single-parent families and that many of these families will be low-income ones (1985). These facts are established. The demand for excellence in education may increase the skills of some high school graduates, but it may also reduce the total number of high school graduates. In Florida, 90 percent of the students who did not pass the competency tests were black (Hodgkinson 1985). Mikulecky (1985, p. 4) notes that fewer than 20 percent of all minority students currently score at the adept level (defined in footnote 1). With increasing numbers of low-income minority students on the horizon it is not too difficult to imagine a scenario in which the demand for educational quality, without sufficient remedial support systems at the high school level, will result in significant reductions in the number of high school graduates. To add to the problems already described, the shifts in financial aid policies appear to be resulting in fewer numbers of black students attending college.

As recently as 1975, the participation rates of black and white stuudents were almost identical (*Statistical Abstracts of the United States* 1985, p. 149). In a short period of time, however, the disparity between whites and blacks has increased so that proportionately fewer black high school graduates are now entering college or university. In 1975, 32 percent of all black persons between the ages of 18 and 24 were enrolled in higher education; by 1983 that percentage had fallen to 27 percent (p. 149). Hispanic high school graduates attend college at the same rate as do white high school graduates. However, Hispanic high school students are more than twice as likely to drop out of high school (*Hispanics: Challenges & Opportunities* 1984). Asian students continue to attend college in large numbers and to perform better academically than minority and white students (Gardner, Robey, & Smith 1985), but they will continue to represent a smaller segment of the high school graduate population than either blacks or Hispanics.

The potential future that emerges from the convergence of demographic and societal trends does not bode well for institutions of higher education.

Minority students, who have traditionally relied on more financial aid and have not been as well prepared for higher education, may increasingly feel discouraged from attending college. This may be the product of academic as well as financial reasons. They may feel discouraged right at a time when their numbers in society are growing and the number of potential nonminority high school graduates is declining. These trends, in light of the fact that the adult student population is not likely to be a source of large numbers of new college students, suggest that a disaggregated analysis of future enrollments would project even greater declines in student enrollments at many colleges and universities. Unless some of these trends are reversed, or institutions of higher education reinvigorate their efforts to attract minority students, the projected decline in college enrollments may turn out to be an optimistic projection.

The Effects of State Policy Trends on Public Institutions

In addition to the trends that may have an impact on the supply of college matriculants, other state policy developments are affecting the ability of individual institutions to attract students. Colorado and Washington have placed enrollment caps on their state institutions (Boyer 1986). In 18 states, state agencies are initiating programmatic and institutional reviews (Boyer and McGuinness 1986). The state coordinating board in New York has actually closed academic programs to reduce duplication and to improve quality. Coordinating boards in several states review and approve all new academic programs. State regulation of enrollments and academic programs has an effect on the ability of the institution to develop academic programs to attract students.

Other states have implemented or are considering incentive funding programs based on the assessment of student learning outcomes. Tennessee, Colorado, New Jersey, and Virginia have established incentive programs based on the ability of state institutions to demonstrate enhanced educational outcomes (Boyer and McGuinness 1986). Other states are beginning to mandate student assessments as a means of facilitating educational improvement at the undergraduate level. The impact of these developments on student enrollments is more difficult to determine. The experiences of institutions such as Northeast Missouri State University and Alverno College would suggest that institutions that are able to document that they facilitate student learning and growth are more successful in attracting students. (In fact, in later sections of this volume the suggestion is made that assessing student outcomes is an important element of an enrollment management system.) State assessment initiatives may actually enhance the ability of institutions to attract and to retain students.

These two categories of demographic and public policy trends have created an external environment as well as institutional environments that require the leadership of colleges and universities to be much more attentive to the factors that shape their enrollments.

THE SEARCH FOR NEW APPROACHES

The convergence of these trends has caused many colleges and universities to invest time and resources in the search for new ways to attract and retain students. In the 1970s institutions began to adopt marketing techniques from private enterprise. Services like the Student Search Service of The College Board came into existence and direct mail began to change the way that admissions offices conducted their business.

Along with renewed interest in student recruitment activities, college administrators also became concerned about retaining students. As early as 1962, Summerskill, in Sanford's book *The American College,* discussed the problem of student attrition. It was not until the 1970s, however, when projections of pending enrollment declines began to be heard (projections of decline had been made by Cartter in 1966 but were generally ignored) that institutions attempted to influence student persistence. Works such as those of Astin (1976), Cope and Hannah (1975), Noel (1978), and Ramist (1981) provided administrators with possible methods of reducing student attrition. In the 1980s projected enrollment declines persist and institutions continue to search for ways to exert more influence over their enrollments. From a strategic planning perspective administrators are seeking the means to move student enrollments from being a resource that is primarily determined by the external environment to a resource that can be more directly influenced by the institution.

One approach being proposed to effect this shift from external determination to one of greater internal influence is that of enrollment management. Enrollment management is an integrated, systems approach to influencing college enrollments. As of yet, however, this concept is not well understood and the elements of an enrollment management system have not been articulated in sufficient detail. A clear understanding of enrollment management is necessary before a system can be put into place.

Defining Enrollment Management

Enrollment management is a more assertive attempt on the part of institutions of higher education to influence their enrollments. It can be defined as:

a process or activity that influences the size, shape and characteristics of a student body by directing institutional efforts in marketing, recruitment, and admissions as well as pricing and financial aid. In addition, the process exerts a significant influence on academic and career advising, the institutional research agenda, orientation, retention studies, and student services. (Hossler 1984, p. 6)

It is not simply a new term for marketing and recruitment activities; it is a complex and holistic approach to analyzing and influencing college enrollments.

On many campuses marketing, admissions, and financial aid activities are conducted in isolation from those of retention programs, and from the general student life programs that play an important role in determining the campus environment. Furthermore, decisions regarding academic issues take place in yet another administrative arena. Institutional norms frequently dictate that different administrators are involved with each of these domains. These norms often prevent campus-wide discussions of the connections between recruitment and pricing, academic programs, and student life. Marketing and aid decisions are often made on the basis of style rather than substance. Academic policies are either determined without regard to student demand or, conversely, dictated by student demand without sufficient consideration of institutional mission and adequate resources. With the decline of "in loco parentis" and the end of student radicalism, student life administrators have become less influential. Yet when academic programs, student life, recruitment, and marketing are viewed as being interrelated, they have a major impact on the image of the institution and its ability to attract and to retain students. Recent research has shown that marketing, recruitment, and pricing policies play an increasingly important role in determining the number and the quality of students as well as the personal characteristics of the institution (Freeman 1984; Jackson 1978; Muston 1984). The quality of student life and the extent to which the institutional environment engages students appear to determine the quality of the student experience, hence affecting recruitment and persistence (Astin 1985; Kuh 1981; Pace 1984).

The quality and range of programs, to a large extent, appear to determine what type of students will be receptive to institutional marketing efforts (Jackson and Chapman 1984; Litten 1986). That is, students do not consider the full range of higher education options when going through the college search process. They appear to consider only certain kinds of institutions. Early in this search process, academic programs appear to be important in determining which institutions will be seriously considered (Hossler 1985).

Scanning the classified section of any issue of the *Chronicle of Higher Education* reveals that the phrase enrollment management is "catching on." It is often, however, simply a new title for admissions officers. On many campuses, the admissions director is being given a raise, a larger budget, and a title such as dean of enrollment management or vice president of enrollment services. Huddleston (1984) has referred to this as admissions management. It should be apparent that an enrollment management system needs to be comprehensive, but frequently the concept is not implemented in a comprehensive manner. A recent survey conducted by The College Board found that a majority of the responding institutions indicated that they were functioning in some form of an enrollment management model, yet fewer than one out of four indicated that financial aid was a part of their model (Novak and Weiss 1985). Fewer than one out of seven of those sampled indicated that their institutions had developed retention plans. If this new approach is to succeed, key elements of the model must be linked together administratively.

Whereas an admissions management system focuses exclusively on marketing and recruitment, an enrollment management system is concerned with student enrollments from the time of the initial inquiry through graduation and post-graduation. Table 1.2 illustrates the continuum from admissions management to enrollment management and suggests the breadth of functions and activities involved.

The Enrollment Management Lens

As Table 1.2 points out, this new model is a comprehensive approach to influencing enrollments. It involves several administrative areas and cuts across traditional organizational boundaries. The ultimate goal of an enrollment management system is to alter the frame of reference that college and university administrators use to view the students as well as the institution. Most admissions officers are accustomed to seeing college students through the lens of the admissions office. This lens looks at how prospective students view the institution and why they are coming. Faculty and student affairs administrators tend to use a different lens to view the student experience. They may view students from the perspective of the classes they teach or from their general involvement with students. Occasionally, one more lens is used, that of student outcomes. This lens is used to understand how students experience the campus and what happens to them after they graduate or leave the institution. Each lens is used to focus the actions and policies of different administrative units on campus. What is usually missing, however, is a holistic view, a wide-angle lens that enables college and university administrators to see the entirety of the college student experience. This wide-angle lens permits them to see students from the time they first consider going to college and their first interaction with the institution, through their student years and the experiences they have in and out of the classroom, to their experiences as alumni. The

Table 1.2. The Enrollment Management Continuum

Admissions Management ———————————→		*Enrollment Management*
Marketing	Marketing and choice	Strategic planning
Recruitment	research	Institutional research
	Recruitment	and evaluation
	Financial aid	Marketing
		Recruitment
		Financial aid
		Academic advising
		and course place-
		ment
		Orientation
		Student retention
		programs
		Learning
		assistance
		Career planning and
		placement
		Student services

enrollment management lens enables administrators to see the entirety of the collegiate experience. Such a viewpoint can inform policy decisions that influence student matriculation, student satisfaction, and student persistence.

A good enrollment management program is not simply a way for colleges and universities to view students. More fundamentally, it helps institutions themselves through the eyes of students. Surveying the attitudes of current students about the campus environment, faculty, administrative offices, curriculum, and extracurricular activities provides direct feedback as to how students are experiencing the institution. This information can assist in the development of more effective policies as well as in evaluating functional areas within the institution. Alumni studies can help colleges determine whether or not they are preparing students for successful and meaningful lives. Frequently alumni will report that they have come to value certain parts of their college experience that they did not appreciate when they were in attendance. Alumni sometimes report that they now realize that there were certain curricular or extracurricular opportunities that were missing from their college experience. This information can have an impact on institutional self-evaluation and policy making. Student college choice and marketing research tells campuses how they are perceived by prospective students and parents; it denies administrators the luxury of seeing the institution the way they would like to see it. As a result faculty and administrators may be forced to accept a more accurate image of the institution, or work to change the campus so that it reflects the kind of image they desire.

This information can be an especially valuable resource for the faculty. Student perceptions of quality are one of the most important determinants of college choice. Thus, academic programs are an important element of an enrollment management system. Faculty typically consider academic policy making to be their domain. Information derived from marketing studies, which demonstrate how prospective students evaluate academic programs, can move academic administrators and faculty to make programmatic changes.

Enrollment Management: A Tightly Coupled System

The enrollment management perspective emphasizes the notion of a systems approach to college enrollments, that is, an effort to systematically link all the policies and functional areas that have an impact upon student enrollments. This perspective represents an attempt to create an organizational system that encourages closer communication and cooperation among the individuals and offices who have an effect upon student matriculation and student persistence. Enrollment management introduces a systems perspective and a more "tightly coupled" organizational structure in an attempt to exert greater institutional influence on college enrollments. In addition it relies on management science to inform institutional policy decisions. It can be viewed as an example of organizational adaptation to the press of the external environment.

The emergence of the enrollment management model is leading many colleges and universities to ask a number of questions. "How can an enrollment management system be developed?" "How does this new approach work?" "Explain it from an administrative perspective." Too often institutions seem to be looking for an ideal model. In order to understand the enrollment management concept, however, it needs to be viewed as an application of systems theory to the area of student enrollments. There is no "ideal" enrollment management system; there is only the application of the systems theory to influencing student enrollments in the unique situation that every campus represents. It is not surprising to discover in Chapters 4 through 7 that our four case studies have put the enrollment management concept to use in different ways. In fact, on two campuses the term enrollment management is not used to describe their activities. In each case what is important to note is that the school has developed a systematic approach to addressing student enrollment-related concerns.

A Systems Approach. Gratz and Salem (1981) describe an organizational system as a set of interrelated or interacting components. Backoff and

Mitnick (1981) state that a system is a set of objects together with relationships between the objects. Systems theory shifts the focus of activities from each separate part to the whole and to the relationships among the parts that comprise the whole. The integration of these parts has a synergistic effect in which the whole becomes greater than the sum of its parts. An enrollment management system attempts to make more evident the linkages among the various activities of the institution that influence enrollments. Linking marketing research to academic planning, for example, may change institutional marketing activities as well as academic planning decisions. When an institution discovers that its engineering program has a poor image among prospective students, academic administrators as well as program faculty are likely to make changes designed to improve the program.

Gratz and Salem (1981) suggest that most college and university administrators understand their own personal responsibilities, but are uncertain how their own roles relate to other roles. By adopting a systems perspective for student enrollments, administrators can begin to see the relationships among the various offices that directly or indirectly influence student enrollments. By bringing the elements of the system together in closer communication, they can enhance each other's effectiveness and minimize the times in which their activities actually impinge upon the goals and objectives of other offices.

In order to build a sound enrollment management system it is essential for those involved to develop the system carefully. Gratz and Salem (1981) state that every system can be identified by its structure, function, and process. Structure refers to the patterns of behavior or activities that occur over time. Function refers to the way the system fulfills its purpose. Process is the way a system changes and evolves over time. Applying these three definitions to an enrollment management system, we can analyze an enrollment management system as follows.

1. Structural analysis—How are the elements of the system arranged? How are offices such as admissions and financial aid encouraged to communicate and cooperate with each other? In what ways are student affairs administrators made "stakeholders" in marketing and recruitment activities? Conversely, is the admissions office clearly linked to student persistence? From another perspective, are the roles of institutional research, evaluation, and strategic planning evident throughout all elements of an enrollment management model?

2. Functional analysis—How effectively does the system achieve its purposes? To what extent are the activity "inputs" of an enrollment management system (recruitment, financial aid dollars, student activ-

ities, retention programs, etc.) producing the desired "outputs" (resulting in student enrollments of the desired size with the desired characteristics)?

3. Process analysis—How does the system change over time? As will be discussed later in this volume, enrollment management systems do change and evolve over time. These changes may strengthen or weaken enrollment management efforts. How and to what extent has an enrollment management model changed over time? Are these changes linked to the people in the system or new developments in the structure of the system? Not all changes will be for the better. Sometimes the departure of a key person can reduce the effectiveness of a system.

For institutions that are just beginning to develop an enrollment management model, the initial step would be to start with a structural analysis. This focuses directly on the interrelationships among offices such as admissions and financial aid; admissions, orientation, and advising; and marketing research and student attrition research. Discussions of structure allow various administrative heads to discuss issues in a less threatening manner. Questions are raised about how offices communicate with each other rather than how effective each office is. By analyzing structure, each office can discuss what they have in common and how they might work together more effectively. For any number of reasons, not all institutions are interested in discussing their enrollments within the context of an enrollment management paradigm. Nevertheless, discussions of structure begin to raise questions related to enrollments, and the potential for exerting more systematic influence on enrollments is enhanced.

Some administrators might argue that, since functional areas such as admissions, orientation, and student activities are already in existence, analyzing an enrollment management system might begin with a functional analysis, that is, the effectiveness of the various offices that comprise an enrollment management system. Until a system has emerged, however (which is likely to be the result of efforts designed to influence oranizational structure), it will be difficult to evaluate the effectiveness of various offices. Efforts to move too quickly to conduct a functional analysis are likely to increase defensive behavior, which will inhibit the degree of openness and cooperation that enrollment management systems require. In addition, the emerging new system may alter the activities of offices, rendering an early functional analysis inaccurate. Therefore a careful functional analysis should follow the development of a structure.

The functional analysis should examine the results of various subcomponents of the system in light of the objectives and resources of the enrollment management system. Have market research efforts enabled the institution to sufficiently target recruitment and aid-awarding activities? To what extent do academic programs facilitate the institution's ability to attract the types of students it wants? Do the orientation and advising programs help students adjust to the environment as well as make the environment more responsive to the expectations of students? These are the kinds of questions that address some of the functions of an enrollment management system. These questions raise issues that require communication and cooperation across functional lines. This is the essence of an effective system.

Process analysis, the monitoring of change in the system, is the last form of evaluation to be undertaken. This assumes that a system exists and that it has been in operation for a period of time. Since few institutions currently have a system in place, there is little need to conduct a process analysis. Over time, however, a process analysis can help enrollment managers to understand how the system is changing. This can help administrators to make adjustments that will strengthen the system as new technologies, new knowledge, and changes in administrative personnel occur over time.

Utilizing a well-defined approach for analyzing an enrollment management system enables institutions to develop administrative structures that are appropriate to the needs of each campus. Such an ongoing process can help to maintain the vitality of student enrollment efforts.

Coupling the System. The other major organizational construct that helps to explain the concept of enrollment management is that of "coupling." Weick (1976) has pointed out that many educational organizations can be described as "loosely coupled." That is, administrative and departmental units operate with a great deal of autonomy. Loosely coupled organizations have difficulty agreeing upon goals, acting consensually, and moving in a united way to achieve organizational purposes. To date, the efforts of colleges and universities to influence their enrollments can best be described as loosely coupled. The activities of such offices as student affairs, admissions, and financial aid have seldom acted in a coordinated fashion and all too often have acted in ways that were counterproductive. Every campus can cite anecdotes that reinforce this point: a student affairs division that decided to alter its housing policies in a manner that will discourage new students from living on campus; a board of trustees' decision to significantly raise tuition rates without input from the offices of admissions, financial aid, and student retention; a financial aid office that decided not to send out aid awards to new students until May 15; the orientation office at an urban campus that is located in a neighborhood perceived as threatening that sent a notice to the homes of all new students about a crime prevention and "street sense" workshop just before these students were to sign their housing contracts. (Needless to say they lost a few students.)

Many students of organizational theory in higher education have come to accept loose coupling as normative. For enrollment managers, the challenge is to create a more tightly coupled system, to bring the offices and administrators who are in a position to influence student enrollment together in a more tightly coupled structure. Again this notion of coupling brings us back to the need to structurally link people, offices, and technologies that can be used to positively influence student enrollments. We will examine some of these potential structures in the next chapter.

Backoff and Mitnick (1981) believe that most administrators look for organizations and systems based on simplicity. They suggest that this is a mistake. Concepts such as the degree of coupling and simplicity should not be viewed as static; they occur along a continuum. Some departments and offices are less tightly coupled than others. Some offices require more complex structures than others. Hall (1981) suggests that while autonomy and loose coupling may go hand in hand for academic departments, most administrative areas are characterized by less autonomy and tighter coupling. The ability to influence student enrollments requires complex systems that do not readily lend themselves to simplicity and that will not be as effective in a loosely coupled structure. Perhaps the best way to describe enrollment management systems is that they are complex, tightly coupled systems.

Management Science: Information Drives the System

College administrators often rely on experience and intuition when making decisions. At times these decisions have proven to be correct and sometimes they have not. The factors that influence stuudent enrollments typically have been poorly understood, and indeed seldom attracted much interest. An accumulation of research in several fields, however, has slowly broadened our understanding of college student enrollments. The groundwork for the enrollment management paradigm has not come from organizational theory, but rather from a convergence of (1) institutional concerns regarding student enrollments, (2) research on student college choice, (3) student–institution fit studies, (4) retention research, and (5) college impact research. Why is this body of research part of the foundation for the enrollment management paradigm? Because, when considered collectively, this literature enables enrollment managers to understand the total student experience, and as a result, many of the factors that influence student enrollments. This knowledge can be effectively used to guide institutional policy-making and enrollment-related activities.

Utilizing research to guide enrollment management activities can best be understood as bringing a management science perspective to these activities. Richard Cyert, president of Carnegie Mellon University, has pointed out that areas such as admissions and financial aid have been among the last areas to utilize management science techniques to increase their effectiveness. Cyert (1981, p. 27) has said of administration and management science that

> management will always remain an art, in part at least, but through an analytic approach the management scientist will be able to reduce the extent of the dependence on "seat of the pants" judgment.

The development of sophisticated research in areas such as student college choice and nonprofit marketing research, the evaluation of the efficacy of financial aid awards and policies, and the application of theory-based student attrition research are examples of management science being brought to bear on enrollment-related issues.

Some examples of these new management science approaches can be found in the work of Bob Lay (formerly of Boston College and now at Suffolk University), who has attempted to use multiple regression techniques to determine whether price thresholds exist for various subpopulations of students. If differing price thresholds do exist, then institutions can more accurately target their financial aid awards. At Oberlin College, David Davis-Van Atta continues to refine his understanding of the Oberlin student market. His application overlap studies help guide Oberlin's recruitment and marketing activities. These studies are not performed to assure institutional survival, but rather to ensure that Oberlin continues to maintain its standing in a very competitive student marketplace. The computer-driven decision information system developed by Jim Gueths and Tom Snider at the University of Wisconsin at Oshkosh is an important element of their enrollment management efforts. COFHE institutions and DePaul University, among others, are starting to use applied research to guide administrative decision making for graduate enrollment-related activities.

Management science, coupling, and organizational systems seem far removed from the concept of enrollment management. Nevertheless, if attempts to understand the nature of an enrollment management system are to succeed, it is concepts such as these that provide an explanation of enrollment management and why it works. A failure to understand these concepts limits administrators to attempts to imitate existing programs. Recognizing the organizational constructs that enable enrollment management models to function frees college and university administrators to develop new systems and unique variations of tightly coupled systems to produce the desired results. Systems theory and Weick's (1976) concept of coupling explain the organizational dimensions of an enrollment management model. Management science explains the need for information to guide the policy decisions of an enrollment management system. Linking the organizational structure with appropriate information leads to increasingly sophisticated questions, solutions, and decisions. This cycle enables institutions to more effectively influence their enrollments.

Chapter 2

Elements and Models

OVERVIEW

In order to develop a comprehensive enrollment management system, a diverse set of functions and activities must be formally or informally linked. Functional areas such as admissions, financial aid, career planning and placement, and new student orientation, as well as less discrete but equally important activities such as outcomes assessments and retention efforts, must be coupled in ways that create communication channels among administrators and faculty involved in these programs.

Two important questions that must be considered when developing an enrollment management system are: What functional and programmatic elements will be a part of the system? and How will the system be organized? These two questions determine the nature and the scope of the system.

THE ESSENTIAL PREREQUISITES

Most planning processes begin with a discussion of the institutional mission statement. Most authors on strategic planning then call for an objective assessment of the external and internal environments. After evaluating the mission in light of the environmental assessments, strategic planning guides usually help the planning team develop realistic goals and objectives that take into consideration both the mission of the institution and its strengths and weaknesses, as well as the external environment.

A college or university that attempts to systematically influence its enrollments should integrate enrollment-related issues into the strategic planning process. Goals and objectives should reflect the size and desired characteristics of the entire enrolled student body, not just entering new students. This focus on the entire student body is what differentiates enrollment management from admissions management.

Once these enrollment-related goals have been articulated, what objectives naturally follow in order to achieve these goals? The objectives should reflect links between areas such as marketing, recruitment, and financial aid. Such linkages should help to answer the following types of questions: What kinds of students are we interested in attracting? Where can we find these students? What do we need to do to attract these students? What do we need to do to retain these students? Academic support services, student life, and the ability levels of enrolled students might be linked with retention goals in the planning process. Linking these areas together should enable campus planners to determine the nature of the student attrition problem so that proactive steps can be taken to alter variables related to student attrition. Institutional research objectives can be tied to longer range goals so that more sophisticated enrollment management activities can take place in the future. For instance, institutions often lack the marketing and student choice research information that will enable them to accurately target their marketing and recruitment activities. Thus, long-range institutional research goals in this area might become part of the planning process. The relationship between academic programs and enrollment goals should also be included. This can occur in two ways. Large departments may determine their own enrollment goals, which in turn determine enrollment management—related strategies for these departments. In other cases smaller institutions may determine that changes in academic programs are necessary in order to achieve overall enrollment goals. In either case academic programs affect enrollments and should be reflected in the planning process. Muston (1984) found a positive relationship between the inclusion of enrollment management goals and strategies in the planning process and success in meeting enrollment- and retention-related goals. Since it is the president and other senior-level administrators who drive the planning process, it is essential that one or more of the senior officers understand the dimensions of an enrollment management system.

It is difficult to have an effective planning process without an ongoing program of institutional research and evaluation. Institutional research provides the data needed to inform the planning process as well as to direct programs in areas such as pricing policies and student attrition. On large campuses, the enrollment division might have its own institutional researcher. Both Northwestern University and Tufts University, for instance, have policy analysts who deal with admissions and financial aid issues. Boston College and Bradley University have full-time researchers in the enrollment management division. On small campuses, the enrollment management function must have access to a centralized institutional research office or be able to draw on the skills of faculty in order to gather necessary data and analyze it. At Oberlin College, the institutional researcher has large portions of his time allocated to enrollment management-related activities.

Efforts in institutional research and evaluation should include student college choice and pricing research and retention studies, as well as assessments of institutional competition, continuing student satisfaction surveys, and student outcomes research. The utility of most of these topics is self-evident. The connection between enrollment management activities and student outcomes research, however, may not be immediately clear. Today's college students and their parents have developed a consumer orientation. Litten and Brodigan (1982) have shown that parents are very interested in the placement records of alumni. They also found that students are concerned about the added economic benefits of attendance. Using the imagery of a lens, outcomes research assists faculty and administrators to see the institution and its effects through the eyes of the student. Outcomes research is increasingly being mandated for many state institutions. This line of research can help institutions to engage in "outcomes-oriented marketing," which may put them in a more favorable position in terms of attracting students. Northeast Missouri State University, for example, has received national attention for its efforts to measure the outcomes of its educational programs. It has recently experienced increases in both the number of applications and in the quality of the entering class. This demonstrates that consumers of higher education are interested in institutions that can demonstrate that they are providing a good education. Willingham's (1985) longitudinal study of students at nine liberal arts colleges, from the time of application to graduation, is also a sound illustration of the utility of outcomes research. By tying together student qualities and characteristics at entrance with outcomes measures such as persistence, involvement, and post-graduation plans of seniors, Willingham demonstrates how enrollment management research can enhance institutional understanding of students and of itself. This can lead to policy decisions that have an effect on student enrollments in addition to improving the quality of student outcomes. The role of institutional research and evaluation is an important prerequisite for effective enrollment management. Focusing on topics ranging from student college choice to student persistence to student outcomes can provide useful information for campus-based enrollment managers.

ATTRACTING APPLICANTS AND MATRICULANTS

Planning and institutional research provide the necessary support systems for an enrollment management program to function. Once this has been done, strategies must be devised that will present the campus in a way that is true to the traditions of the institution and that will make it attractive to prospective students. This usually falls to the admissions office or the marketing office. However, tuition levels and financial aid policies also have an effect on who applies and who attends. Effective marketing programs are data driven; questions such as who attends college, why they attend, and why they choose one institution over another will guide individual marketing efforts. Litten (1986) compares marketing activities that are not research based to witchcraft. On many campuses, the use of marketing and social science research for the study of student college choice and marketing activities is still in its infancy. The results of researchers such as David Brodigan, Randall Chapman, Larry Litten, John Maguire, and David Davis-Van Atta demonstrate that institutions can use this emerging area of research to gain a better understanding of the nature of their student markets. This understanding enables institutions of higher education to more accurately target their marketing and recruitment activities.

Unlike some elements of an enrollment management system, such as student persistence, which cross virtually all institutional boundaries, marketing and recruitment are typically the domain of one specific office—the admissions office. Although the administrative responsibilities are well defined, the nature of the process will vary. Two-year colleges direct their attention to a well-defined local market, so in that sense their task appears to be more manageable than that of four-year colleges who draw from a wider geographical area. On the other hand, the two-year college student market is characterized by a great deal of diversity, whereas four-year institutions will usually have a more homogeneous student market. The degree of diversity in terms of geographic distribution and student background characteristics dictates different marketing strategies. Two-year institutions must struggle with cost-effective methods of reaching market segments with diverse interests and needs. This may require a multitude of different brochures and other printed material, each designed to speak to a different audience. Four-year institutions, although appealing to a more homogeneous population, must still develop different tactics for various market segments while grappling with the additional variable of geographic dispersion. Questions of cost effectiveness take on different dimensions as the geographic dispersion of the institution's markets increases.

Pricing and financial aid policies are integrally linked with marketing and recruitment efforts. Tuition levels play an important role in determining whether or not an institution will continue to be considered as an educational option during the search phase of the college choice process (Hossler 1984; Jackson 1982). Once students form a choice set, the role of financial aid packages becomes more important. Ideally the financial aid office should make aid awards in a timely manner in conjunction with other "courtship" activities organized by the admissions office. The impact of aid when coordinated with other courtship activities such as special scholarship banquets, letters from the president, campus visits, and other forms of special recognition has sometimes been overlooked, or at least poorly coordinated by four-year colleges and universities. This is especially true of community colleges who have tended to rely on low tuition as the primary vehicle for attracting students. Many two-year colleges continue to overlook the importance of aid and courtship despite the fact that their costs are rising and that evidence shows that community college students are the most cost-sensitive college attenders (Manski and Wise 1983; Zucker and Nazari-Robati 1982). Nevertheless, the most important aspects of tuition and aid policies in attracting matriculants are pricing strategies that enable the institution to be perceived as being within the cost range of the potential student market segments the college is trying to attract.

Enrollment management programs also need to take into consideration the inherent tensions between issues of access and equity when juxtaposed with the emphasis placed on the bottom line—the total number of students enrolled. The historic purpose of financial aid has been to enable low-income but otherwise qualified applicants to attend a college or university. The increasing use of "no-need" merit scholarships at a time when total financial aid resources are holding steady or even declining raises ethical dilemmas that enrollment managers should not overlook in the name of effectiveness. Although some observers have argued that there is no tension between merit- and need-based aid, it seems doubtful that no-need awarding strategies can be implemented without reducing the amount of aid available to less advantaged students, thus reducing access and choice.

On a more pragmatic level two concerns should be kept in mind. First, a larger percentage of future high school students will be less advantaged minority students. Unless policy makers at the national, state, and institutional level are careful, they may create an environment that discourages these students from pursuing higher education. This would have negative consequences for student enrollments at many colleges and universities. Second, research has raised serious questions about the efficacy of no-need scholarships. Many single-institution studies have concluded that "no-need" money does have a positive influence on student matriculation decisions, but many of these campus-based studies suffer from conceptual and design flaws. Two multicampus studies conducted by Freeman (1984) and by Jackson and Chapman (1984), which are less flawed, conclude that "no-need" aid has only modest and in some cases negative effects on students' matriculation decisions. Jackson and Chapman state that it would require several thousand dollars to enable an institution to move itself from a second to a first choice institution. Freeman notes that institutional courtship activities accompanying the aid offers may be more important than the actual amount of the award. These studies suggest that merit-based aid programs should be modest unless they have convincing evidence that larger amounts of aid result in greater numbers of students. A critical design question for institutions that are attempting to study the impact of their "no-need" aid awards should be, Would we have attracted these students anyway?

The admissions and financial aid offices are important elements of an enrollment management system. They represent the admissions management subsystem of an enrollment management system. The admissions subsystem model (Tables 2.1 and 2.2) visually displays the connections among the factors that influence student matriculation. The admissions subsystem model also includes guidelines to assist enrollment managers as they work through the questions raised by the model. As the admissions subsystem model shows, however, marketing, recruitment, pricing, and aid do not represent a total enrollment management system.

INFLUENCING THE COLLEGE EXPERIENCE

Admissions management efforts stop once students matriculate. For enrollment management models, the focus of attention shifts to that of the students' college experiences. An integrated enrollment management plan attempts to facilitate a smooth transition into college as well as being concerned with the total student experience during each student's tenure at the institution. This is not to suggest that campus administrators and faculty have not been concerned with student life. Using the analogy of the enrollment management lens, the enrollment management paradigm requires that we not only view the college student experience from the perspective of the admissions office, the student affairs office, or the faculty, but also that we view the experience as the students perceive it. A systems model requires admissions officers to be concerned about issues of student–institution fit and student affairs officers to be more accountable for the ways in which they influence the attractiveness of the campus environment. Bean (1986), for example, suggests that admissions officers be evaluated on the basis of how many matriculants persist rather than on the number of students who are recruited. Astin (1985) recommends that student affairs administrators think through how they facilitate student involvement in all facets of the college experience. The importance of the faculty begins with the relationship between program quality and college selection and continues throughout the college years as evidenced by the positive impact that formal and informal faculty contact has upon the goals and aspirations of students (Pascarella 1985).

Table 2.1. Admissions Subsystem Model

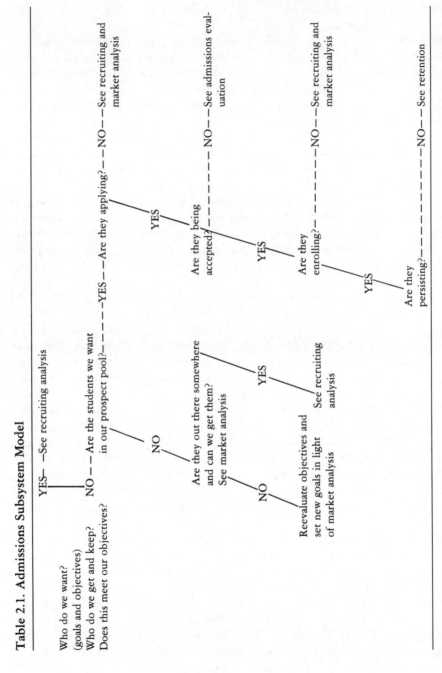

Adapted from Novak and Weiss (1985b).

Orientation programs should be designed to help students adjust to the intellectual and social norms of the campus, along with the physical layout of the campus. For example, Feldman and Newcomb (1969) conclude that most students arrive with only a vague notion of what the campus is really like. They expect to have close relationships with faculty and believe that their academic endeavors will be their primary source of satisfaction. On how many campuses is this the case? Again Feldman and Newcomb indicate that for most students, once they arrive, peers become their primary reference group and source of satisfaction. If this is the case, how do enrollment managers design orientation programs that introduce students to the realities of the environment without presenting a picture that is so divergent from their expectations that they become disappointed and consider leaving the institution? Pascarella (1985) recommends that orientation be viewed as an opportunity for "anticipatory socialization," that is, creating new student expectations that more closely approximate campus environment and norms. In this way students are more likely to find meaning and satisfaction in their college environment. Noel (1985) has noted that most students who leave an institution during the first year make the decision to do so early in their first semester. Such findings suggest that orientation programs can play an important role in retention programs. Pascarella reports that participation had a small but significant indirect positive effect on student persistence.

Almost all campuses have an orientation program, but not all orientation programs receive the careful scrutiny and attention from senior campus administrators that they merit. The initial expectation of close contact with faculty is especially problematic for community colleges and some larger four-year institutions. Both types of institutions frequently use professional counselors or academic advisers who are not discipline-based faculty members for their orientation programs. This makes it difficult to meet an important set of student expectations during the first critical weeks of college. To address this problem, orientation programs could adopt a twofold strategy. First, orientation directors could attempt to present a more accurate image of student–faculty interaction. Second, they could attempt to increase faculty involvement in orientation and academic advising during the first weeks of school in order to facilitate student adjustment. Such a strategy would combine the concept of anticipatory socialization with efforts to alter, or manage, the institutional environment.

Along with orientation, quality academic advising is also important for new students. Advising and orientation frequently overlap. For many students their first advising session takes place during orientation. Academic advising is a natural place to involve the faculty with students. Several campuses have begun to take advantage of the linkages between orientation

Table 2.2. Admissions Planning Overview

Question	Analysis	Data
1. Who do we want? Who do we get and keep? Does this meet our objectives?	Profile of enrollees and persisters Compare same to objectives	Academic abilities (test scores, grades, coursework units, predicted ability?) Demographics (geography, ethnic, gender) Academic interests (major, degree) Personal attributes (leadership, athletic ability) Admissions status
2. Are the students we want in our prospect pool?	Compare prospects to objectives	Same as above
3. Are they out there somewhere and can we get them? (see market analysis for more detail)	Market potential Image analysis Competition analysis Program and pricing analysis Institutional resources and priorities	Same as above plus: student surveys info on competitors national, regional, state, ACT, College Board data population data and enrollment forecasting programs
4. Are they applying? If NO:	Compare appliers to objectives Look at appliers vs. prospects who are not appliers (look at competition and image analysis)	Same as question 1 Other data that would differentiate appliers from nonappliers
5. Are they being admitted?	Compare admitted to those appliers not admitted (look at admissions policy and procedures)	Other data that would differentiate admitted from nonadmitted
6. Are they enrolling? If NO:	Compare enrolled to objectives Compare enrollers to those who were admitted but did not enroll Look at competition analysis, image analysis, financial aid packaging and costs	Same as question 1 Other data that would differentiate enrollers from nonenrollers

Marketing

1. How many prospects, appliers, and accepted students do we need to get in order to meet our enrollment objectives?
2. Are the students we want out there?
3. Will they be attracted to our institution?
   What's our image?
   Does this match our strengths and weaknesses?
   Does this meet the students' interests/ needs? (program offerings, cost/pricing policy, student services, and special programs)
4. Do we have the resources to get them? [financial aid packaging, programmatic changes required to meet unmet students' interests or needs (for example, a new program in computer science, dormitories), recruiting budget and staff, etc.]
   If NO: Reevaluate admissions goals and objectives
   If YES: See recruiting analysis

   1. Marketing surveys
   2. Overlap studies
   3. Competition analysis

   1. Competitive analysis of aid and awarding policies
   2. Internal assessment of aid resources and awarding policies

Recruiting

1. How many prospects, appliers, and accepted students do we need in order to meet our enrollment objectives? (yields)
2. Where are they? (define, refine primary, secondary, and tertiary markets)
3. What do they need/want? (survey of students) (in addition to the descriptive information implied in goals and objectives, such as majors, data may include housing, financial aid, extra- and co-curricular activities)
4. Do we offer what they want? (survey of current students)
5. Do they know it? (image analysis, compare appliers vs. nonappliers, etc.)
6. Do we tell them we have it? (publications analysis)

and advising to develop extended orientation/advising programs. The well-publicized "University 101" course at the University of South Carolina is an example of this. Using faculty in these extended orientation/advising programs or in small freshman seminars (these seminars can be assigned so that each student's adviser is teaching his or her seminar) is another way of creating a good vehicle for advising and encouraging student–faculty interaction.

For most students, their first interactions with their new environment revolve around academic advising, course placement, and new student orientation. As Mikulecky's research indicates (see Chapter 1), the diversity of today's college students has resulted in wide variations in the interests, experiences, and skills that students bring with them upon matriculation. This is especially true of two-year colleges and open-admission institutions where some matriculants will enter with minimal academic skills whereas others would be eligible for honors programs at almost any college or university. This has increased the importance of academic advising and course placement. A comprehensive enrollment management plan should include academic assessment tools that increase the likelihood of appropriate course placement. Helping students to select the courses that will challenge but not overwhelm them is another important function of orientation and advising during the critical freshman year. Students who do not fare well academically are less likely to persist. The College Board and American College Testing Program offer placement instruments and many institutions have developed their own placement examinations. Careful attention to course placement can be an important enrollment management strategy. Appropriate course placement can help ease the transition to college.

Successful integration into the campus environment should have a positive impact upon student persistence. Student retention research and programs are an important part of any enrollment management plan. Thus far this discussion of an integrated enrollment management system has attempted to explain programmatic activities in the order in which they drive the system. As with planning and research, however, it is difficult to ascertain precisely when effective retention efforts begin. Do they begin with early warning systems or exit interviews? Do they start with good classroom instruction or with marketing and recruitment programs that emphasize the importance of student–institution fit?

The question of when retention programs begin is difficult to answer. It is also hard to identify who is responsible for student retention programs. Retention cuts across many functional areas and divisions within the institution. It is precisely because of the many organizational variables influencing student attrition that student retention research and programming should be assigned to a specific administrative office. The committee approach, which is used on many campuses, almost ensures that retention will not receive adequate attention. As Kemerer, Baldridge, and Green (1982) point out, committees are seldom able to influence institutional policies and programs. The importance of student attrition in maintaining enrollments suggests that it needs to be the assigned responsibility of a specific individual, just as admissions or financial aid is the assigned task of identifiable administrators. This ensures that data will be collected and programs will be planned, implemented, and evaluated. Without specific administrative attention, student attrition is lost in a maze of committees and discussions. Issues affecting retention are seldom clearly identified or addressed. Committees may still be valuable in order to sensitize administrators and faculty to retention-related issues, but direct administrative responsibility should ensure that the concern receives continuous attention. The retention officer should not be held personally accountable for attrition rates; the issue is too complex for any individual to control. Nevertheless, creating an administrative office to deal with student retention can make sure that the institution as a whole continues to deal with issues related to student persistence. The retention officer should be an integral part of the enrollment management system.

Student attrition has been a concern on many campuses for several years. There is little evidence that most colleges and universities have moved beyond determining their attrition rate. This is the result of a failure to evaluate retention-related activities. Many institutional administrators have read the retention literature and developed generalized retention programs, but few have taken the time to determine whether or not their efforts are effective. Much like market research, theory-driven attrition research has demonstrated that different subpopulations persist or withdraw for different reasons. Thus any generalized approach may not meet the needs of specific institutions. Enrollment managers need to develop institutional specific retention programs that are then evaluated. Such an approach might be described as the "second generation" of retention activities.

Along with areas such as orientation and advising, the learning assistance office needs to be a part of retention efforts. Many colleges will continue to admit some underprepared students. In order to help these students succeed academically, campuses have established learning assistance offices. These offices typically offer a wide range of services, which may include study skills workshops, reading assistance, writing labs, test taking workshops, and tutoring in specific subject areas. Professionals in this area should be considered part of the enrollment management staff and included in the communication network. The admissions officer usually identifies marginal students during the admissions process. As a result they are in the best position to inform the learning assistance office of the particular academic needs of these students. Completing the circular flow of information, learning assistance offices are often charged with monitoring the academic success of students. This places them in a unique position to provide continual feedback to the admissions office regarding student success. If few marginally admitted students are succeeding, then the institution may not be spending its recruiting and financial aid dollars wisely. In addition, staff time in the learning assistance center may be better spent elsewhere. This office can be a link between the admissions officer and the student retention function.

Up to this point, this section has focused on issues related to student fit and student retention. Just as there is an admissions subsystem component of an enrollment management system, enrollment managers should include a student fit/retention subsystem model as part of a comprehensive enrollment management plan. This student fit/retention subsystem (Tables 2.3 and 2.4) enables enrollment managers to address issues related to student–institution fit and persistence.

Career concerns have become an important consideration for college students from the time they select an institution to the time they graduate. They are keenly aware of the competitive nature of the job market. Career planning and placement can be viewed as a bridge between areas such as student satisfaction or student persistence and student outcomes.

Institutions that are perceived as helping to place their graduates in good jobs after graduation will not only be in a better position to attract new students, but also to retain current students. Part of the job turnover model of student retention used by Bean (1980; 1983) posits that the practical value of a college degree—the likelihood of getting a desirable job after graduation—has a positive effect on student persistence. Developing a strong career planning and placement operation should not only help students in establishing linkages between their academic and vocational goals, but in attracting students as well.

In addition, Litten and Brodigan (1982) note that parents of prospective students are interested in job placement information. One of the expected individual outcomes of higher education is that of good employment and increased productivity for college graduates. Colleges and universities need to track the placement records and career patterns of their graduates in order to better understand the impact of their educational offerings. An effective placement office should also enhance marketing and recruitment efforts because current high school students as well as adult students are more likely to attend an institution with a good placement reputation. It is difficult to imagine an enrollment management plan that did not include a strong career planning and placement officer.

Table 2.3. Student Fit/Retention Subsystem Model

What is our retention rate?

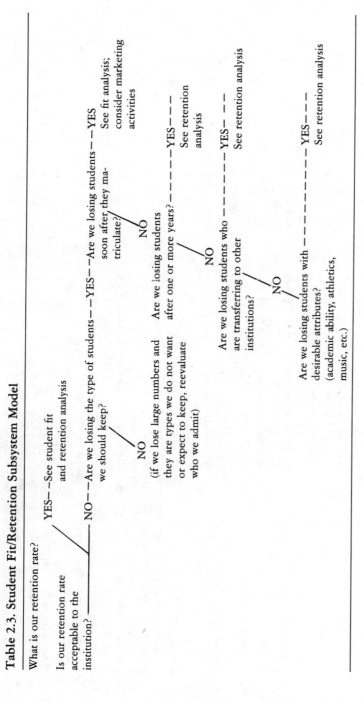

Is our retention rate
acceptable to the
institution? ——— YES—— See student fit
and retention analysis

——— NO——Are we losing the type of students——YES——Are we losing students——YES
we should keep? soon after they ma-
triculate? See fit analysis;
consider marketing
activities

NO (if we lose large numbers and NO
they are types we do not want
or expect to keep, reevaluate Are we losing students
who we admit) after one or more years?——————YES————
See retention
analysis

NO

Are we losing students who ——————YES— — —
are transferring to other
institutions? See retention analysis

NO

Are we losing students with ——————————YES———
desirable attributes?
(academic ability, athletics, See retention analysis
music, etc.)

Table 2.4. Student Fit/Retention Planning Overview

Questions	Analysis	Data
1. Are we keeping those we enroll?	Comparison of matriculants and non-persisters	Enrolled student files and registrar's files of those not registered
2. Are we keeping those we would expect and want to keep?	Compare ability levels of persisters and non-persisters Compare academic programs Compare background characteristics Compare academic and career plans	High school and college GPA Major Sex, race, socioeconomic status Financial aid awards Distance from home Clarity of future plans
3. How long are we keeping our enrolled students?	Determine persistence rates for each class and for transfers Determine graduation rates for 4 and 5 years	Registrar's files
4. Why do students stay or leave?	Compare responses to questions	Surveys, exit interviews of graduates and dropouts
5. Are our nonpersisters involved in the institution?	Profile of grade-point average (GPA), activities involvement, work on campus, etc.	Surveys, registrar's files, student affairs records, campus employment records

Student Fit Analysis

1. Do we accurately portray the institution to prospective new students?
2. How do new students perceive the campus environment?
3. How do returning students perceive the campus environment?
4. What is the degree of fit between student expectations of the campus environment and the actual campus environment?
    How do we help students adjust to the environment?
    How can we change the environment to meet student expectations?

Student Retention Analysis

1. How do we encourage student involvement in the institution?
2. How do we facilitate student success at the institution?
3. How do we identify dropout-prone populations?
4. How do we develop intervention programs for potential dropouts?
5. How do we evaluate our retention programs?

Thus far this discussion of the college experience has focused on specific tasks and functions within an enrollment management system. Equally important, but more complex, is the entire array of student services found on most campuses. Functions such as student activities, career planning, learning assistance, and orientation tend to be found on most college and university campuses. They are typically part of the student affairs division. Depending on such variables as whether or not the institution is residential, activities, intramural and intercollegiate athletics, residence life, and Greek affairs can greatly enhance the quality of campus life. In addition to being rewarding, Astin (1985) asserts that student involvement in curricular as well as co-curricular and extracurricular activities while attending college determines the quality of student outcomes as well as influencing student persistence. The emphasis that Astin (1985) and Pace (1984) give to student involvement provides a strong theoretical underpinning for strategies to facilitate student development. Students who are involved, satisfied, and growing are more likely to persist and be advocates of the campus after graduation. By enabling student affairs administrators to infer growth from involvement, the theory of student involvement also provides more readily measurable indices of student growth. Student affairs officers, through careful planning and evaluation, can develop programs that encourage student involvement. The student affairs division has an important role in determining levels of student satisfaction and student outcomes. From an enrollment management systems perspective this brings us back to the imagery of the wide-angle lens, which enables us to see and understand the entire college experience.

Our discussion of the elements of an enrollment management system began with planning and research and moved next to the marketing and recruiting of students. It then examined the student college experience. This brings the discussion to graduation, the point at which the student becomes an alumnus of the institution. A comprehensive enrollment management plan, however, should not stop with graduation. Student outcome studies should include regular assessments of alumni. Their experiences and attitudes can provide institutions with useful information, thus emphasizing again the prerequisites of planning and research. As shown in Tables 2.5 and 2.6, to understand the student experience and then develop informed policies that attempt to enhance those educational outcomes the institution finds desirable as well as to minimize undesirable outcomes requires sound institutional research and strategic planning. To complete the final subsystem of a comprehensive enrollment management model, a student outcomes subsystem model is presented. In some sense, "subsystem" is the wrong word for student outcomes. A campus that engages in systematic studies of its outcomes is analyzing the nature of the entire

Table 2.5. Student Outcomes Subsystem Model

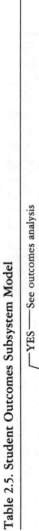

Are our students having the kind of educational experience we want them to have?

— YES —— See outcomes analysis

— NO —— Are we satisfied with the outcomes of attending this institution?

—— NO —— Are our students having the kind of in-class and out-of-class experiences we want them to have?

—— NO —— See current student outcomes analysis

YES

Are our students satisfied with their experiences inside and outside of the classroom?

—— NO —— See current student outcomes analysis

YES

Have our alumni been well prepared for their careers and leisure time?

—— NO —— See alumni outcomes analysis

Are our students satisfied with their educational experiences?

Are our alumni satisfied with their educational experiences?

institution and its students—this is hardly a subsystem. In order to work with parallel constructs within the context of an enrollment management paradigm, however, the student outcomes subsystem is outlined as an aid for enrollment managers as they attempt to analyze institutional outcomes.

The Faculty

Organizational issues and administrative activities have thus far been the primary focus of this chapter. Although faculty have been referred to at various points, their role in an enrollment management system has not been addressed. This section does not fit neatly within the organizational structure developed in the first part of this chapter, but faculty do play an important role and it is a mistake for any enrollment manager not to consider their role.

An enrollment management system is an administrative structure. Colleges and universities, however, have two organizational structures: the more hierarchical and relatively tightly coupled administrative structures and the flat, more autonomous and loosely coupled faculty structures. It would be a tactical mistake, and impossible on most campuses, to attempt to dictate policy to faculty. Yet, faculty have a direct impact on student enrollments in a variety of ways. Perhaps first and foremost, the academic quality of programs is the most important factor in determining where a student will go to college (Jackson and Chapman 1984). It is difficult, however, for administrators to speak to issues of academic quality. At best they are likely to be disregarded and at worst administrators will alienate themselves from the faculty, thus reducing their effectiveness. As has already been pointed out at the beginning of this chapter, this is where market research, current student surveys, and alumni questionnaires can provide a mirror for faculty to see their programs as others see them. Using this mirror can create an impetus for changes in academic programs that come from within the faculty, which would be impossible for administrators to require of the faculty.

Student–faculty interaction appears to have a powerful impact on student outcomes and student persistence. Enrollment managers should play an educative role with the faculty in this area. Through colloquia, short position papers, newsletters, and faculty development seminars, administrators should continually educate the faculty about the potential effects they can have on students both in and out of the classroom. On many campuses the connection between enrollments and institutional health are already understood by the faculty. On these campuses acquainting them with research that documents the impact of faculty upon students and the role of academic programs in college choice is likely to create a receptive audience for enrollment management activities.

Table 2.6. Student Outcomes Planning Overview

Questions	Analysis	Data
1. Are our students having the kind of educational experience we want them to have?	Comparison of institutional goals with student achievements	Standardized assessment tools; sophomore-year comprehensive examinations; pre- and post-tests
a. Gaining general knowledge? (liberal learning)		
b. Gaining special knowledge?	Comparison of student achievements with national data bases	Standardized graduate school admission examinations; certification examinations; graduate school acceptance rates; job placement rates
c. Involvement in co-curricular and extracurricular activities?	Comparison of institutional goals in noncontent areas with students' involvement in these areas	Local surveys; standardized college student experience instruments
2. Are our students satisfied with their educational experience?		
a. Curricular experience?	Profiles of student satisfaction with instruction, content, library, major, etc.	Local surveys; exit interviews
b. Co-curricular and extracurricular experience?	Profiles of student satisfaction with lectures, student activities, intramurals and intercollegiate athletics, etc.	Local surveys; exit interviews
3. Are our alumni satisfied with their educational experience?		
a. Career training?	Profiles of alumni satisfaction with job training	Local surveys; standardized questionnaires
b. Preparation for leisure time?	Profiles of alumni satisfaction with development of avocational interests	Local surveys; standardized questionnaires
c. General life-style?	Profiles of alumni satisfaction with preparation for productive life and citizenship	Local surveys; standardized questionnaires

Current Student Outcomes Analysis

1. What are the liberal learning sensibilities we want our students to develop?

2. How do our curricular, co-curricular, and extracurricular programs work together to facilitate the kinds of liberal learning we hope to impart?

3. What goals do we have for our students for the development of specialized skills and knowledge?

4. How do our curricular, co-curricular, and extracurricular programs work together to facilitate the kinds of specialized skills or learning we want to develop?

5. Are our current students satisfied with their classroom experiences and their academic majors?

6. Are our current students satisfied with the co-curricular and extracurricular programs the institution offers?

Alumni Outcomes Analysis

1. Are our alumni able to find jobs or enter graduate schools in the fields of their choice?

2. Do our alumni believe the institution has helped them to develop avocations?

3. Are our alumni satisfied with their college experience?

Using research to guide faculty involvement can also help prioritize the use of faculty time. On many campuses the faculty are already being asked to help recruit students, to be excellent advisers, and to be involved in all facets of campus life in order to encourage student–faculty interaction. In addition, they are asked to develop high-quality academic programs and be excellent teachers. It is little wonder that the faculty at some institutions are feeling burned-out. An enrollment management plan should realistically assess the role of the faculty and try to develop incentives to encourage faculty involvement at important points. Administrators should also take into consideration the differing strengths of faculty members. It is not uncommon to hear admissions officers praising one faculty member for his willingness to write or call prospective students, while criticizing another faculty member, who has been developing an outstanding academic program, because he or she does not write letters. The faculty member developing the academic program may actually be doing more to attract and retain students.

A Comprehensive System

A comprehensive enrollment management plan should address the administrative structure of the institution as well as the role of the faculty. It should adopt a view of the student experience that links new student matriculation, new student adaptation, student persistence, and student outcomes. The factors that influence enrollments, however, are far too complex to be controlled or managed by any "cookbook" approach to institutional management. Organizational models are beginning to emerge, nevertheless, which can be adapted to fit the needs of individual institutions. These models offer a range of structures and vary widely in the degree to which they couple the elements of an enrollment management system.

ORGANIZATIONAL MODELS

The discussion of systems, coupling, and the components of enrollment management provides the context for an examination of four models. These four models are drawn from the work of Kemerer, Baldridge, and Green (1982).[1] They have in some sense become archetypal models that are used to describe most ongoing institutional enrollment management programs. These models were cited in my first examination of enrollment manage-

1. See *Strategies for Effective Enrollment Management* (Kemerer, Baldridge, and Green 1982) for a more complete discussion of these models.

Table 2.7. Four Enrollment Management Models

Low	Loose	Enrollment Management Committee
Organizational restructuring required	Degree of organizational coupling	Enrollment Management Coordinator
		Enrollment Management Matrix System
High	Tight	
		Division of Enrollment Management

ment (Hossler 1984); however, they should be revisited in order to help illustrate some of the concepts that have already been presented in this chapter. In addition, Chapters 3 through 6 will present institutional case studies that have utilized one or more variations of these models. In order to analyze these case studies, the four archetypal enrollment management models will be discussed here.

The four models are presented in Table 2.7. Each model has its own strengths and weaknesses. They vary greatly on several dimensions, and as we shall see in the case studies, there is variability in the ways that each institution puts a given model into operation.

The Enrollment Management Committee

The enrollment management committee is often the initial campus response to enrollment-related problems. The committee may begin with a focus on marketing and admissions, student retention, or with a holistic view of student enrollments. As noted in Kemerer, Baldridge, and Green (1982), committee membership usually includes some key faculty members, middle management administrators from areas such as admissions, financial aid, and student affairs, and perhaps a senior officer, such as the vice president for student affairs or the vice president of academic affairs.

The committee's charge is frequently unclear. Charges such as "to examine enrollment problems on the campus" or "to look into institutional marketing and recruitment activities" are not unusual. The committee begins with unclear goals and is comprised primarily of members who have little knowledge about the complex set of factors that influences student enrollments. In addition, the membership of committees changes regularly; this makes it difficult for them to move forward and follow through on any agenda that might develop. Coupled with these drawbacks is the fact that most committees have no formal authority and often have no direct way to influence institutional policy making. Such a descripton would seem to suggest that the committee approach has little to offer. This is not necessarily the case.

The committee approach can be a good vehicle for educating a large group of people about enrollment-related issues. Since many members do not have a background in these areas, they start at a basic level and learn a good deal about such issues as market segments, need versus merit aid, and student persistence. These committee members then become advocates of enrollment-related issues and resources. An effective committee can help activate a campus. In a situation where there is little support for changing the status quo, a committee is also a "safe" way to address institutional norms and examine problems. In some settings, the committee may be the only viable mechanism for exploring enrollment management issues.

While it would be difficult to describe the enrollment management committee as a tightly coupled system, it can be viewed as the first step toward creating an enrollment management system. On many campuses, even creating a committee begins the process of coupling enrollment-related issues. With an understanding of the potential of the committee approach, there are certain guidelines that are likely to enhance the effectiveness of such committees. First, try to make sure the enrollment management committee has a clear charge that indicates some of the first steps the committee should take. Plan to educate the committee members in a systematic fashion. Begin with basic issues and then develop the more complex themes. Include on the committee one or two senior administrators. This will ensure that the issues and concerns related to enrollment management will be heard in senior-level administrative councils.

The Enrollment Management Coordinator

The enrollment management coordinator is most frequently a mid-level administrator and often the director of admissions (Kemerer, Baldridge, and Green 1982). Typically the coordinator is assigned responsibilities for coordinating and monitoring the enrollment management activities of the institution. On many campuses, the term enrollment management may be used, but in reality the coordinator oversees only admissions and financial aid.

As Kemerer, Baldridge, and Green point out, the weakness of this approach is that mid-level administrators seldom have the influence and authority to change administrative practices and procedures. Perhaps equally important, this person may be separated from senior level administrators by one or more layers of administrative bureaucracy. As a result the enrollment management agenda may not be heard by those managers with the authority to change structures and allocate resources.

The coordinator's role can be effective, however, if the coordinator has good communication skills, is persuasive, and is well regarded in the organization. In addition, if the coordinator has a proven record of effectiveness on the campus, he or she may have already accrued idiosyncratic leadership credit. In this way the coordinator can exercise leadership in the organization despite the fact that he or she may lack formal institutional authority.

Appointing an enrollment management coordinator moves the institution in the direction of a more tightly coupled enrollment management system. Also, by being responsible for these activities, this administrator is more likely to begin to develop a systematic data base, which can later become the basis for more informed policy decisions. Like the committee approach, the coordinator's position may be the most effective way to move in certain situations. When there is a high level of mistrust and turfdom among the principal offices that should be involved in enrollment management efforts, and these offices report to different vice presidents, the committee or coordinating function may be the only politically viable alternative. Any move toward a more centralized approach might create so much hostility and resistance that even the best conceived structure would never be able to function. The coordinating function also has one benefit over the enrollment management committee: it does make someone accountable for at least monitoring enrollment management activities. This role can even be strengthened if the coordinator is assigned to report directly to a senior level administrator.

The Enrollment Management Matrix

The enrollment management matrix moves colleges and universities one step closer to a centralized and tightly coupled system. In the matrix model, the administrators who have the most direct influence on student enrollments are brought together regularly under the direction of a senior level administrator. All of these middle managers will not report directly to this senior administrator, but as with most organizations with a hierarchical pattern, those with lower status tend to be more responsive to those with more status. The senior level manager functions somewhat like the enrollment management coordinator, only with more power.

The advantages of this model are several. Most important, a senior level administrator now takes direct responsibility for enrollment management programs. This is likely to ensure more impact on organizational structure and resources. Cooperation and communication among the appropriate offices will increase. The linkages between institutional research and policy making become more tightly coupled. Finally, the head of this matrix model will become enmeshed in all elements of an enrollment management system. This process is likely to educate the administrator and create a well-informed advocate in senior level administrative circles.

This model does have some disadvantages as well. As suggested by Kemerer, Baldridge, and Green, in most circumstances the senior administrator may not have the time that enrollment-related issues require. As a result the system may become slow and ineffective. In addition, this is a more centralized enrollment management system. Creating such a system may have political reverberations that reduce the effectiveness of enrollment management activities. In some situations, the time required to educate the senior level administrator may use up valuable time for all those involved.

The matrix model may be most appropriate on campuses where there is a history of people reporting to more than one administrator. It may also be more effective in situations in which there is a perceived problem and the organization believes that it must act swiftly. On large campuses a *highly* centralized system may not be desirable because of the size and complexities of each school or division within the institution. In such cases, a matrix model may be the most advantageous approach. The model can also be an evolutionary step that helps to break down organizational barriers that have prevented the development of a more centralized system.

The Enrollment Management Division

The enrollment management division represents the most centralized and tightly coupled enrollment management system. In this model all of the major offices connected with enrollment management efforts are brought together directly under the administrative authority of one senior level administrator. The advantages of such a system appeal to most administrators. Each of the principal components of the system can be both directed and coordinated by one vice president. In this model issues of cooperation, communication, and resource allocation can be dealt with from a system-wide perspective. In addition, the vice president speaks with formal authority on enrollment issues in all policy decisions.

The principal liability of this model is that of administrative turf and organizational politics. Rarely do other vice presidents gladly relinquish control over offices that are part of their administrative portfolio. In many colleges and universities, philosophical differences make it difficult for areas such as career planning or student activities to find themselves reporting to someone who carries the title of enrollment manager. Such a title doesn't sound very "developmental." In any case, even presidential fiat does not easily change existing patterns and politics. As a result the potential benefits and liabilities of an enrollment management division should be weighed carefully before implementing this model.

The centralized division can probably be implemented most rapidly in situations in which an enrollment crisis is perceived. Under these circumstances organizational barriers are more fluid and change is accomplished more easily. The enrollment management division can also be put into place when the organization has been slowly moving toward this model for some period of time. Creating an enrollment management division under these circumstances is then viewed as the natural culmination of a set of developmental trends.

Eclecticism and Creativity

Each of these models has assets and liabilities for individual institutions. It is important to note that no single model may best fit the needs of a specific campus. In addition, if we refer back to the concept of a process analysis of enrollment management systems, we will likely find that the system does change over time.

Enrollment management systems that started from the activities of a committee often evolve over time through the coordinator model to the matrix model. On some campuses the coordinator and committee structures may exist side by side. The coordinator works with the committee in educating the college community on enrollment-related issues and influencing institutional policy, and at the same time continues to monitor and to facilitate the development of new enrollment management activities. The case studies that come later illustrate that there is more than one organizational structure that institutions can use to influence their enrollments. These cases studies will also demonstrate that systems do indeed change and evolve over time.

ON SYSTEMS AND SUBSTANCE

Developing an enrollment management system model can assist colleges and universities in their efforts to exert more influence over their student enrollments. The enrollment management lens can only be used to improve our vision and enable administrators to make more informed decisions. It does not allow us to actually manage our enrollments.The ability to make more informed decisions regarding student enrollments, however, should not be taken lightly. Better vision and more informed decisions can help us to come closer to our goals.

It must always be kept in mind, however, that enrollment management models focus on systems within the institution, rather than the substance within the institution. The two should not be confused or overlooked. Student attrition studies may indicate that many students at a church-related college find the environment too restrictive. Market research may reveal that a selective liberal arts college could serve new markets by developing intensive weekend programs for underprepared adult learners. A state university, historically committed to access and equal opportunity, may believe that it could attract more students and enhance its image by shifting from a need-based to a merit-based financial aid philosophy. These examples point out the potential tensions between some expedient enrollment management goals and wider questions of institutional history and mission. The resolution of these tensions is complex: to err on the side of technocratic efficiency in the long run may harm the institution and widespread use of ill-conceived educational practices can diminish public confidence in the entire system of American higher education.

Chapter 3

Developing an Enrollment Management System

On many campuses there is interest in developing an effective enrollment management system. The impetus for changing the organizational structure to implement an enrollment management system varies across institutions. On many campuses admissions officers and financial aid administrators who see that institutional efforts to manage their enrollments are not as tightly coupled as they could be are attempting to bring about change. At other colleges and universities student affairs administrators are leading efforts to institute enrollment management systems. At still other institutions the press for change is coming from faculty, institutional research officers, academic administrators, and presidents. Some examples of the varied background of these "change agents" will be seen in the case studies presented in Chapters 4 through 7.

A frequent problem for would-be change agents, however, is determining the best strategies to utilize on individual campuses. Lindquist (1978, p. 18) states that "colleges and universities may be great places to get all kinds of things started, but they are terrible places to get them implemented." There is a large body of literature on organizational change that can be applied to higher education. However, it often errs on the side of assuming that there is one best way to bring about change. Baldridge (1983) has suggested that there is no theory of change for educational organizations. Organizational change literature will be reviewed here, with special emphasis on three change models: an accrual or evolutionary model of change, a rational or planned change model, and a crisis-oriented or transformational change model. After reviewing each model, a contingency framework will be proposed that posits that effective change strategies are dependent on organizational and environmental variables. These internal and external variables may suggest very different change strategies at different points in the life of an organization.

For enrollment managers, the implications of these change models demonstrate that just as there is a variety of potential enrollment management models, there is also more than one approach to facilitating change in institutions of higher education. Frequently would-be change agents, after being exposed to a new idea, will ask, "How can I implement this on my campus?" Unless those desiring change are willing to deal with the complexities of both the concept itself and changes in the institution that will be required, such a question is naive. Faculty and administrators wishing to develop enrollment management models at their colleges or universities will need to carefully analyze their institutions to determine the most effective enrollment management system, as well as look for the most appropriate strategies for bringing about the changes needed to implement the system.

THE ACCRUAL CHANGE MODEL

To long-time members of most stable educational organizations, substantive change seems to take place slowly if at all. These perceptions are at least partially correct. In stable organizations there is change, but it does take place slowly. Rapid change in stable colleges and universities does not usually occur. The decentralized and loosely coupled nature of institutions of higher education makes it difficult for administrators to bring about rapid changes. Organizational inertia, existing structures, and the normal resistance to change on the part of individuals militate against attempts to alter the institution.

This does not mean, however, that change does not take place in stable institutions. A potentially useful way to study organizational change in colleges and universities is to examine organizational charts over a long period of time. New positions, new titles, and new reporting relationships often reflect changes in the institution. Not all alterations in organizational charts represent genuine change; some may simply reflect titles with higher status for administrators who continue to perform the same tasks. Other alterations in the organizational chart, however, do represent real changes. Creating the position of policy analyst for the admissions office or retention officer in the student affairs division, changing the title of the chief student affairs officer from that of vice president of student affairs to vice president of student affairs and enrollment planning, or asking the dean of enrollment management to report directly to the president are often indicative of organizational changes.

The study of job descriptions and organizational charts can be a useful method to analyze change in stable colleges and universities. It is difficult, however, to study evolutionary change or slow change. Organizational change does not lend itself easily to experimental designs; thus it needs to be studied in vivo. Case studies are a common method for studying change, but few researchers are willing to spend the time it takes to study slow accretionary change in colleges and universities. As a result, little has been documented about this form of change.

Miner and Estler (1985) present an accrual model of job mobility that is helpful in efforts to understand slow or evolutionary institutional change. They observe that many college and university administrators move up through the administrative ranks not as the result of taking unfilled well-defined jobs, but rather as the result of new positions being created to fit the individual. This is produced by the interaction between individual abilities, organizational issues, and environmental pressures. The product of these three interacting variables is often tailor-made jobs or idiosyncratic positions that reflect the unique needs of individual institutions and the specialized skills of people in them. The accrual model in a stable environment is the most likely model to succeed in introducing change. In an accrual model, an administrator first accrues responsibility, skills, or knowledge that exceeds the normal job requirements. These responsibilities evolve into duties that become expected of the individual, and eventually are formally recognized and incorporated into the organizational structure.

Miner and Estler outline the factors that affect the probability of accrual job mobility, factors that will be adapted for use in an accrual model of change. They identify environmental turbulence as an external factor that can facilitate change through accrual. This environmental turbulence is not of such great magnitude that it threatens the organization, but it is sufficient to be noticed by institutional leaders. In response, administrators search for alternatives to the perceived threat.

Organizational factors also affect the accrual change process. Problems leading to change must be viewed as important, they must be visible, and they must appear to be difficult to solve. The importance and visibility of the problem ensures that the organization will attend to the problem, while the distasteful nature of the issue discourages the use of existing structures to respond to the problem (few administrators want to tackle "this one"). In addition, those accruing the responsibility for this organizational change must have access to alliances and personal visibility within the institution. Finally, any potential change must be consistent with the values of the campus.

These environmental and organizational factors also interact with individual factors. Administrators who have determined that the accrual model of change is best suited to the current situation must be assertive, persistent, and open to risk taking. In addition, Miner and Estler's findings suggest that an accrual change agent must be perceived as competent and display intellectual curiosity.

The accrual model of change has clear implications for those wishing to develop an enrollment management system in stable institutions. Developing an enrollment management system in a stable institution will require patience. In most cases the campus will not perceive this problem in the same way it currently directs its recruitment, financial aid, and student retention activities. As a result there will be little organizational support for moving to an enrollment management approach. Most campuses, however, are at least concerned about demographic projections and their potential impact on the size or quality of student enrollments. Thus environmental turbulence is present and the issue has some visibility.

Aspiring enrollment managers will require visibility and respect from the campus community. Any plans they develop will have to be flexible in view of the varying responses their ideas will receive. When using the accrual model it is better to flood the institution with ideas and to be persistent about them. As Cohen and March (1974) point out, administrators are usually remembered for their ideas that are implemented; no one remembers the ideas that were never even tried. In addition, in colleges and universities there is no such thing as a final decision.

Part of the strategy of the accrual change process should be an educative one. Since there is no mandate for an enrollment management system, those attempting to implement the system must continually attempt to educate key administrators and faculty about the complexities of attracting and retaining students and make them aware of potential approaches to effectively managing these complexities. This strategy helps to build alliances and establishes the merit of the enrollment management model.

Of the various enrollment management models proposed by Kemerer, Baldridge, and Green (1982), the enrollment management committee is the most appropriate model to start with when using an accrual change process. It does not require a major response on the part of the institution, but it does provide a forum for the campus to explore enrollment-related issues. It can help to educate participants and to build alliances with other administrators and faculty. Establishing an enrollment management committee cannot be a short-term goal. Since there is no impetus for change, change agents in an accrual model will have to build a base over a long period of time in order to establish a committee. Would-be enrollment managers should try to position themselves so that they can play a key role on the committee, but not necessarily chair it. The best person to chair the committee may be a senior level administrator, who then frequently becomes an advocate for more tightly coupled, enrollment-related issues and activities.

In some situations the position of enrollment management coordinator may also be an appropriate long-term goal for an accrual change model. The coordinator is in a good position to be visible and assertive, and to flood the campus with enrollment management ideas. The loosely structured role of a coordinator also facilitates flexible and creative responses, which are required when there is no perceived need for developing an enrollment management system. The lack of strong support for change often means that those attempting to implement change must "take what they can get" in the way of change rather than seeking what they perceive to be the single best organizational response.

The accrual model of change offers the most realistic approach to change on many campuses. It is a realistic approach that takes into consideration the resistance to change among individuals and institutional structures. It can result in organizational change when there is little perceived need or support for change; in many ways it is a subversive model of change. Change agents are attempting to introduce change when most members of the organization do not perceive a need for change. The accrual model, however, does require change agents who are patient and committed to the institution for long periods of time. Those pursuing an accrual change process have to be very flexible, realizing that the final product of their change efforts may look very different from how they envisioned it. Change agents using this change model must constantly react to opportunities, both anticipated and unanticipated. Strategies are more a matter of reflex than of planned action. Opportunism perhaps best characterizes this approach to change.

THE PLANNED CHANGE MODEL

The planned or rational model of change is the most widely prescribed change strategy. There are a wealth of descriptions and case studies of planned change strategies. The literature on planned change will be reviewed and applied to implementing enrollment management systems.

Planned change models assume that institutions are rational and that a systematic approach to planning and implementing change will result in the implementation of the desired state. Nordvall (1982) notes that rational planning models make the following assumptions:

1. Change comes about when rational people are convinced by the arguments presented to them to implement the change.
2. Good ideas for change need to be presented in convincing ways.
3. Good change ideas are derived from scientific research.
4. Organizations act rationally (a belief widely held despite contradictory evidence).

Unlike the accrual model of change, institutions using a planned or rational change model are usually more intentional about their desire to change. There exists a perceived need to change, which is usually the result of some internal or external environmental threats on the horizon. These perceived threats are typically not immediate, but they are visible enough to cause the institution to begin seeking new adaptive strategies to cope with them. In response to the threat, campus administrators seek responses that will insulate the institution from the potential problems or even turn the problem into a competitive advantage. A rational, planned change approach is often selected to implement any needed change in the organization. Planned change strategies permit the participation of administrators and faculty, a prerequisite in most colleges and universities. They also appear to produce a very logical and reasoned response to perceived problems.

Most rational planning models propose a step-by-step process for implementing change.[1] The first step in most models involves unfreezing the institution. All organizations have a level of equilibrium that maintains the status quo. Those desiring change must therefore disturb the equilibrium so that the organization is prepared to consider new ideas. Unfreezing can be accomplished by tactics such as making members of the organization aware of new approaches that are producing more effective results elsewhere, having people within the institution attend a conference on a new concept, or bringing people together within the organization who are dissatisfied with the status quo to discuss how things might be changed. Any one of these tactics, as well as others, can be used to introduce the desire for change within the institution.

Following the unfreezing of the organization, the rational planning model calls for the consideration of possible alternatives. That is, those involved in attempting to introduce the change begin to discuss and to consider possible alternatives to the status quo and what would be needed to implement each one. Both factors that would facilitate as well as inhibit implementation of each alternative are analyzed. The result of this process is that the list of possible alternatives is reduced. Only one or two possible courses of action will appear to be feasible and desirable. From this short list an appropriate course of action is selected.

Selecting a course of action leads to planning the implementation of the desired change. Lippitt, Watson, and Westley (1958) point out that, during this action planning stage, some of those who appeared to be interested in change will drop out. This should be expected as part of the sorting-out process that reveals who is really interested in the change and who is not.

---

1. For a more complete discussion of rational change models see *The Change Agent's Guide to Innovation in Education,* 1973, by Ronald G. Havelock; *Strategies for Change,* 1978, by Jack Lindquist; *The Process of Change in Higher Education Institutions,* 1982, by Robert C. Nordvall.

The planning process should include some interim evaluation check points that are built into the change strategy. These evaluations enable the change agents to determine whether or not they are moving toward the achievement of their goals.

Once the change strategy is developed, the plan is implemented. The action implementation stage should include evaluation check points. These mid-process evaluation points may provide feedback, which in turn leads to some alterations in the implementation process. It should be noted that new options may emerge during the process that are even more attractive, or new obstacles may emerge that require scaling back the original plan.

If all of the other steps have been successful, the change strategy is implemented. The entire rational change process, however, is not completed. Change agents must be sure to develop new support systems to ensure that the new change becomes part of the equilibrium of the organization. If this does not occur, then the change will not persist.

This step-by-step model of rational change has been refined to include new considerations as they have emerged in the literature on change. Nordvall (1982) has included concepts such as social networks, problem solving, and the political model of change at various points in the rational change model. Social interaction and problem solving strategies can be used durng the unfreezing, the consideration of alternatives, and the action planning stages. Social interaction theories focus on how new ideas are disseminated within organizations. Problem solving examines how the receiver of new ideas comes to feel the need for change.

Political models deal with issues of power, authority, and coalitions within organizations. They serve as a correction for rational models because they help to explain why good rational ideas sometimes fail. They can fail because existing bureaucratic and personal values strongly favor the status quo. Thus, bringing about change is likely to involve conflict and compromise as would-be change agents interact with the existing norms and values of the campus.

Authority is an important issue in its own right in rational planning models. Successful planned change strategies need not be developed by leaders of the organization. In fact, those individuals will often not be the source of innovation and change. Daft and Becker (1978) conclude that every change process requires an initiator or "idea champion," someone who is persistent, persuasive, and willing to push others to follow through and implement the recommended change. Leadership, however, is also required to implement change. Support from administrative leaders serves as a catalyst to bring about change; this support facilitates the development of coalitions and draws attention to issues that may influence the change process (Lindquist 1978; Saario 1979).

Since the dominant managerial paradigm by which most college and university administrators operate is one of rationality, it is not surprising that many attempting to implement an enrollment management system will utilize a rational change model. For would-be enrollment managers the first step may be garnering the support of a senior level administrator of the institution. This provides the environment necessary to begin to openly work on the development of an enrollment management system. The approval of a senior administrator will not necessarily guarantee success. In most institutional settings, not even the president can act by administrative fiat. Even in cases where this occurs, the cooperation and support of offices such as financial aid or career planning and the assistance of the faculty may not be forthcoming. This will diminish the effectiveness of enrollment management efforts. Those attempting to use the rational change model still need to work through each step of the process. Creating a perceived need to move to an enrollment management system, developing a plan to establish the system, implementing the system, and establishing the support to maintain a smoothly functioning system will be necessary.

In situations in which strong administrative support exists for developing an enrollment management system, there are more options in terms of organizational structure than when an accrual strategy is being utilized. One of the major advantages of the planned change model over the accrual model is that the change process itself, because it is more intentional, can occur at a faster pace. Faster, however, does not mean quickly. Fullan (1982), in a review of studies of change in educational settings, indicates that most change processes took at least two years to complete. The accrual change model will take even longer and is more difficult to evaluate. Since the members of the organization never declare an intent to change, there are no goals with which to compare the results of the change process (individuals involved in an accrual process may have had some goals, but these were not a formal part of the goals of the organization).

Rational approaches to change have some limitations that should be evident at this point. First, organizations are not always rational, so attempts to work through the change process rationally may not succeed if the would-be change agents are not flexible and attentive to resistance and to new issues as they emerge. Planned change efforts typically rely on participation from a variety of administrators and faculty. This process can be time consuming and produce results that are far removed from the initial goals of the desired change. Planned change models, nevertheless, probably offer the most desirable approach to change when compared with the accrual model or the transformational model discussed in the next section.

Using a rational change model, the initial steps for developing an enrollment management plan are likely to be completed by a committee. In that case some form of enrollment management committee may be the first enrollment management model to emerge. The committee may eventually produce a set of recommendations that suggest some sort of administrative structure. Since the problem that initiated the change process seldom presents an immediate threat to the institution, it will be difficult to generate enough support to bring about major administrative restructuring. This suggests that the enrollment management coordinator or the matrix model may be the most appropriate models for institutions using a planned change strategy. These two enrollment management models have an impact on staffing and organizational structure so that they give visibility and credibility to enrollment-related issues. On the other hand, they do not require the major restructuring necessary for the creation of an enrollment management division.

A TRANSFORMATIONAL CHANGE MODEL

One of the variables that has been used to help direct this discussion of change strategies is the degree to which the institution is threatened by the external environment. In the accrual model, the organization is stable and perceives few threats to the areas in which potential enrollment managers would like to see change occur. In the planned change model, the organization is basically stable, but administrative leaders perceive a potential threat and are seeking possible solutions to insulate the organization from the threat. In the third model of change, the transformational model, these variables of threat and stability have moved further along the continuum. The organization perceives a major threat to its stability and thus seeks change quickly in order to respond to the situation. The term "transformation" is meant to convey rapid change in which some characteristics of the institution are altered in significant ways. Some organizational theorists have argued that colleges and universities find themselves in this situation because they failed to recognize the threat and engage in adaptive behavior earlier. This argument is not relevant for this chapter; the focus is not how institutions get to this point, but rather how they respond once they acknowledge their situation.

The transformational model of change draws heavily on studies of how institutions respond to crisis. Kerchner and Schuster (1982) observe that colleges and universities that believe they are in a crisis situation initiate adaptive change strategies much more rapidly than might normally be possible. They state that "crisis is risky, but under certain conditions it can be transformed into an instrument for doing good" (p. 121). The principal force for change in this situation is the fear that the situation will become worse if the campus does not act. In such situations the normal bureaucratic channels and consultative processes of the institution can be suspended. Shorter and more tightly coupled communication channels are established. The problem(s) perceived to be the cause of the crisis receive unlimited attention and energy.

Kerchner and Schuster identify variables such as financial and human resources, leadership credibility, and the degree to which the crisis is visible to all members of the campus as determinants of strategy for transformational change. The most favorable position for change agents attempting to bring about transformational change is in leadership roles with high credibility, a high level of resources, and a very visible crisis. In this situation the change agent can declare a crisis and proceed with an active and rapid search for possible changes that will ameliorate the situation.

When any one of the above criteria are missing, the strategy becomes more complex and the results more difficult to predict. If the crisis is not visible to others, change agents will have to devise strategies to make the problem visible before they can declare a crisis and then respond to it. If change agents lack credibility, they may not be believed if they declare a crisis or they may be blamed if they are believed. Neither situation is desirable for those hoping to bring about change as a result of the crisis. If the organization lacks financial and human resources, often referred to as organizational slack, then the range of change strategies may be limited. This would reduce an institution's ability to find a viable solution to the crisis.

The ability to suspend normal operating procedures in order to accomplish transformational change is potentially attractive to many administrators who have attempted to institute change only to be thwarted by the inertia of the status quo. This makes the use of crisis a potentially useful tool to bring about transformational change. It should be noted that in the previous two change models mid-level administrators (with support from senior level administrators) might be the major actors in bringing about change. In the transformational approach to change, however, a senior level administrator, most often the president, will have to lead the campus through the change process if it is to be successful. Given the leadership of a senior level administrator, Kerchner and Schuster (1982) offer some tactical guidelines for instituting transformational change.

1. The declaration of a crisis cannot be half-hearted; it must be highly visible and unequivocal.
2. The crisis must be managed conspicuously with dramatic results.
3. Make use of outside experts to dramatize the problem.

4. Bind yourself to a future that would be too distasteful if permitted to occur.
5. Make use of a crisis council; the council should be the best minds, not just the right titles.
6. The crisis council should be empowered to act decisively, by-passing normal channels when necessary.

For enrollment managers the transformational change model is most likely to be useful when the institution perceives a crisis in student enrollments, one in which enrollments threaten the stability and health of the institution. It is a problem that affects everyone on the campus because it threatens their job security. To implement an enrollment management model in a crisis situation will probably require that the president take the lead in declaring the crisis and restructuring the institution. Those interested in developing an enrollment management system may find themselves a part of the crisis council and play a role in creating the system. Ultimately, however, the president will have to be viewed as the principal actor in creating the new enrollment management system.

In a crisis situation, issues and solutions become more tightly linked and decision making is more centralized. For these reasons the matrix or enrollment management division is the most likely organizational structure to emerge from a transformational change. Symbolic actions are as important as substantive actions during a crisis; therefore, simply creating an enrollment management committee or hiring an enrollment management coordinator will be perceived as equivocal actions, not decisive enough to deal with the magnitude of the problem. From an evolutionary perspective, a crisis council (a committee) is likely to assign a senior level administrator or a middle manager with high status to direct the efforts of an informal matrix enrollment management model. The next step is likely to be either a formalized matrix model or an enrollment management division.

Transformational change strategies can be very appealing because they permit rapid change. They require decisive actions from institutional leaders. Kerchner and Schuster, in fact, suggest that it may be advantageous for college and university leaders to manipulate a situation so that a crisis becomes visible or at least seems very close on the horizon. An impending crisis permits rapid change to be accomplished. Transformational change strategies, however, also hold the greatest risk for senior administrators. If they are not believed when they declare a crisis, their credibility is lessened and their ability to be effective leaders decreases. If they declare a crisis and then do not successfully manage it, they are likely to lose not only their credibility, but their jobs as well. Thus, while transformational change strategies offer some of the greatest opportunities for administrators who desire change, they also hold the greatest risks for administrators and institutions.

ORGANIZATIONAL SIZE AND COMPLEXITY

Each enrollment management model and change strategy has been examined from an institution-wide perspective. In addition, variables such as institutional size, institutional complexity, and the degree of centralization in the governance system and the degree of state control should also be taken into consideration when developing an enrollment management model as well as selecting the appropriate change strategy. Large institutions tend to be more decentralized and more complex. Tightly coupled enrollment management models such as the enrollment management division may be difficult to implement in universities where there are several large and autonomous schools or colleges. In such settings it may be more appropriate to pursue an enrollment management matrix model, a coordinator, or even a committee at the university level. In each college or school, however, there might be a coordinator or even something resembling an enrollment management division that is attentive to the goals and objectives of the individual school. Schools of music, education, and engineering might have an associate dean charged with enrollment management-related activities. These associate deans might be part of a university-wide enrollment management committee or matrix structure. The goal of each school would be to attract the desired number of students with the optimal mix of skills and talents. Change strategies in large, complex universities will normally follow accrual models or planned change models. It is unlikely that these institutions will ever face enrollment crises that threaten their stability, although state coordinating boards may mandate policies that have a major impact on the enrollments of some public institutions. In this case, the transformational model may be the desired change model. Individual schools may also face threats to their funding levels as a result of enrollment declines that cause them to change in a transformational manner and develop their own enrollment management models irrespective of what is occurring in the university as a whole.

In smaller, less complex institutions, the full range of models and change strategies can be considered. In smaller institutions historical patterns of governance are an important consideration. In institutions that have a history of strong leadership and less participative management, more centralized enrollment management models can be implemented using a planned change model. If, however, senior administrators do not see a need for developing an enrollment management system, then individual middle managers will have to follow an accrual change strategy. In colleges and universities that have a history of participative decision making, change strategies will usually have to follow accrual or rational models. Enrollment management models that emerge in participative institutions are initially more likely to be a committee, coordinator, or matrix model unless there is a crisis at hand.

A CONTINUUM OF MODELS

For both change models and enrollment management models it should be evident that selecting the appropriate system and using the best strategy to implement that system is a complex interactive process. The selection of both the enrollment management system and the appropriate change strategy depends on a variety of factors such as the size and governance structure of the institution, the stability of the institution, the degree of "ownership" senior administrators have in developing an enrollment management system, and the extent to which the campus believes it should be concerned about student enrollments. Thus, both change models and enrollment management models should be viewed as existing along continuums.

Enrollment management models exist along a continuum of coupling as shown in Chapter 2. These models can also be seen as evolutionary. A college or university may begin with a committee and then move to more centralized and tightly coupled models over time. An enrollment management coordinator can become part of a matrix model and later be appointed to lead a newly created enrollment management division.

Change models also exist along a continuum. The continuum varies according to such factors as the external environment, institutional slack, and leadership support for change. The situational change model presented in Figure 3.1 depicts the interactional nature of effective change strategies.

Figure 3.1 shows that the type of change strategy selected has an impact on the scope of the change and the strategies used by the change agent(s). In an accrual model there is little intention on the part of the institution to bring about change. There is a great deal of intent in transformational change efforts, but in an atmosphere where quick decisive action is needed issues may be oversimplified and important implications of decisions overlooked. In slow accrual change situations the change agent must almost be subversive and Machiavellian in attempting to introduce new ideas and initiate new programs. In planned change models, change agents need to engage in constant anticipatory testing, attempting to determine what the potential outcomes may be of various activities. Because change involves

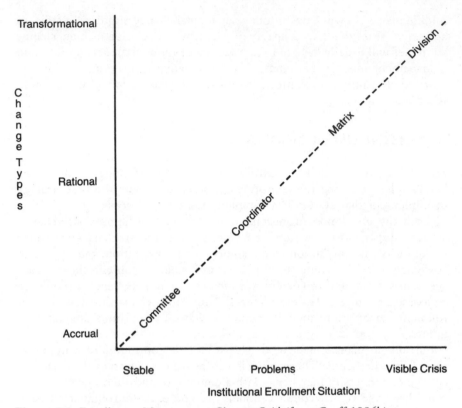

Figure 3.1. Enrollment Management Change Grid (from Graff 1986b).

other people, there is also a need to attend to the means of change, that is, the political issues that will arise during the process. In transformational change situations, change agents must act decisively and be perceived as strong leaders who "can make things happen."

In Figure 3.1, the three change models have been paired with the severity of enrollment problems to suggest which of the four enrollment management models may be the most appropriate. As the severity of the enrollment problem intensifies, the more likely it is that a centralized enrollment management model will be selected. Figure 3.1 would not hold true for all situations, but is descriptive of the developments in many institutions.

Perhaps the most important concept to keep in mind for those attempting to implement an enrollment management system is that change needs to be considered as a dependent as well as an independent variable. Most discussions of change have assumed that once a strategy is selected, the strategy then determines the outcomes (thus change is viewed as an independent variable and the outcomes of change are the dependent variables). When issues such as institutional stability, organizational slack, and environmental threats are taken into consideration, change strategies become dependent variables, that is, the change strategies are determined by these factors. These environmental factors then interact with the change strategy and other issues to determine the success of the change efforts. This is a fundamental shift from the way most administrators have viewed the change process. By making the change strategy a dependent variable, administrators may be able to more accurately identify the most effective approach to bring about change.

Viewing change in such a manner makes the task of an enrollment manager more difficult and complex, but oversimplified views of change are likely to result in misdirected and unsuccessful change efforts. Fullan (1982) concludes that most attempts at change in educational settings do indeed fail. Perhaps they fail because an overly simplistic approach to change has been used. Enrollment management systems for colleges and universities can be developed. Doing so requires paying attention to the institution and its environment, as well as to enrollment management models and appropriate change strategies. The next four chapters will illustrate the diverse models and paths institutions have taken to develop their systems. As you read through each chapter it may be a good test of your observational powers to attempt to analyze the change strategies employed and the types of enrollment management models put into place.

Chapter 4

A Case Study: Johnson County Community College

William Chatham

INTRODUCTION

Johnson County Community College is a two-year public institution located in Overland Park, Kansas, which is a suburban area of Kansas City, Missouri. Johnson County, Kansas, had a population of 266,489 in the 1980 census and is expected to increase to at least 320,000 by the year 2000.

The college opened in the fall of 1969 with an enrollment of 1,390. As a nonselective, open-admission institution, the college experienced steady enrollment gains through its short 15-year history and enrolled 8,103 students in fall 1984. With a headcount of over 8,500 students in fall 1985, Johnson County Community College, the largest of the 19 public community colleges in Kansas, is the fourth largest institution of higher education in the state of Kansas. Only the University of Kansas, Kansas State University, and Wichita State University are larger.

The college has a diverse curriculum, offering courses and programs in liberal arts and vocational areas. The primary emphasis of the college, however, is the transfer curriculum. Approximately 60 percent of the students plan to complete a four-year degree, taking their first year or two at Johnson County Community College and then transferring to a four-year college or university to complete their degrees. Follow-up studies conducted by the college with the cooperation of four-year colleges and universities suggest that Johnson County students perform at an academic

WILLIAM CHATHAM has been involved in the admissions, records, and financial aid profession for 15 years at both private four-year and public two-year colleges. He has been with Johnson County Community College for the last 10 years.

level equal to or above that of students who take all of their classes at four-year colleges or universities.

The college has a strong financial base, with 57 percent of its support derived from property taxes. With a total assessed valuation of over one billion dollars, and without the burden of voter approval for increases in mil rates, the college is in an enviable position for generating operating funds.

WHY ENROLLMENT MANAGEMENT?

It would seem that a college with a remarkable growth rate, located in a major suburban population area and possessing a healthy budget, would not have many enrollment problems. Indeed, the enrollment problems of the college are in fact minor, with an actual decline of less than 1 percent from fall 1983 to fall 1984. However, a larger decline in credit hour generation, the basis for all state aid, was experienced from 1983 to 1984. This decline in actual credit hours generated in fall 1984 fell short of the total estimated by the administration of the college.

For the entire academic year of 1984–85, the college missed its credit hour projection by 12,609 credit hours or 8.6 percent. Missing enrollment projections for budget purposes by this much helped focus attention on the enrollment of students and the services necessary to recruit successfully in a very competitive market. The president of the college expressed concern about the shortfall in credit hour generation and what could be done to stem the tide and to become more aggressive in the recruitment and retention of students.

Historically, the college cannot be characterized as an aggressive recruiter of students. The college has never employed a full-time admissions counselor, has never participated in The College Board's Student Search Service, and has never done any extensive follow up on prospective students. The college has, in the past, taken a very passive role in the recruitment of students, relying primarily on the bulk mailing of credit class schedules to all residents of the county each semester.

What recruitment efforts the college does extend are directed primarily in the student services division. Even in the student services area, recruitment efforts are disjointed, since visitations to high schools are organized by the admissions office, orientation programs are organized by the counseling center, and the college catalog and other student-oriented publications are coordinated by the dean of students. Faculty involvement in recruitment efforts is mostly nonexistent with the exception of the allied health areas of the nursing and dental hygiene programs.

The organizational structure of the student services area does not lend itself to integrated efforts in the recruitment of students. Coordination of recruitment efforts between all areas of student services is lacking and no single person is responsible or held accountable for ensuring that the college operates a dynamic and aggressive student recruitment program.

PRESIDENTIAL TASK FORCE ON ENROLLMENT MANAGEMENT

In July 1984, the director of admissions, records and financial aid participated in a national conference on enrollment management. Upon returning to the campus at the completion of the conference, the director met informally with the president of the college, who was expressing concern about the decline in the early enrollment of students for the fall 1984 term and was asking what could be done about the problem. The director also expressed his frustration that all the components needed for an aggressive recruitment and enrollment program at the college were spread throughout the organization, making coordination difficult. A discussion was held regarding other colleges' handling of this situation. The president had read about the new philosophy and had also noticed a larger demand in recent job postings in national publications for directors, deans, or vice presidents of enrollment management.

In response to the president's request for further information about enrollment management, the director prepared a brief synopsis of the proceedings of the national enrollment management conference. In addition, a copy of all of the conference papers was provided.

After the materials were reviewed, the president became convinced that an enrollment management philosophy could be implemented at Johnson County Community College. All the components of a sound enrollment management program were available at the college. What was needed was an organizational effort to bring these components together.

Working through the existing structure of the college appeared to be the best organizational approach. Involving the president, the vice president for academic affairs, the dean of instruction, and the dean of students would ensure the open lines of communication that would be required to have a successful effort. The president felt the best approach would be to appoint a task force, reporting directly to him, composed of key faculty and administrators. The emphasis of the task force would be to conduct a self-study of all the areas of the college having contact with students and examine what was being done to maximize the enrollment and retention of students.

The director of admissions, records and financial aid would chair the presidential task force and the membership would be determined by the director, the academic vice president, the academic dean, the dean of students, and the president. At a joint meeting it was decided that the task force would include one faculty member from each of the college's academic departments and one member from each of the student service areas that were primarily responsible for the student admissions process. The areas of admissions and records, financial aid, and counseling were also included in the group. In addition, the support service areas of the college were to be represented. The areas included were the business office, security, institutional research, and public information. Including representatives from all of the areas mentioned resulted in 14 members on the task force. In order to stress administrative commitment to the faculty members participating in the project, the academic dean would also be a task force member.

The charge to the task force was to analyze everything the college was currently doing to facilitate the enrollment potential of the college. It was to be a total institutional approach, realizing that every area of the college is responsible for working with students. Additionally, all areas of the college would be given the opportunity to suggest improvements that could be made in serving students to help maintain and increase enrollments.

The membership of the task force was completed using input from the six academic departments. The goal in selecting faculty members was to identify those perceived as leaders within their respective departments and who had outstanding student evaluations of their classroom performance.

Other members of the task force were identified according to their abilities to relate to students and to the general public. Staff members with good communication skills, high degrees of empathy, and a strong service philosophy were chosen to serve on the task force.

THE RESPONSIBILITIES OF THE TASK FORCE

The first responsibility of the task force was to become familiar with the concept of enrollment management. The director of admissions gave a lengthy overview using some readily accessible resources. A series of six videotapes titled *The Enrollment Management Lecture Series,* by John Maguire (1984), was made available to the task force. Copies of *Enrollment Management: An Integrated Approach,* by Don Hossler (1984), were also shared with the group. As with all committees, some members would take their task seriously and review all the materials, and others would not. Based on this assumption, a general overview of the materials was given to the group.

The members of the group were able to grasp the basic concepts of enrollment management after a few meetings. The next phase of the project was to compare the philosophical and practical aspects of enrollment management and examine how they would fit at Johnson County Community College. This would be determined by completing an extensive institutional self-study.

INSTITUTIONAL SELF-STUDY

To prepare the groups, the office of institutional research provided abstracts of several ongoing research projects regularly completed by the college. The projects included various surveys that measured student and community satisfaction with the college and its programs, and community attitudes toward higher education.

The task force was divided into groups. Each group was assigned self-study projects in areas related to enrollment management at Johnson County Community College. These self-study topics included:

Admissions and records
Financial aid
Counseling and student development
Special services for handicapped students
All six academic divisions
Business office
Safety and security
Student activities
Food service
Bookstore

To ensure continuity among all the self-studies, the following outline was prepared for use by each of the subgroups.

A. Mission of service area
    Goals
    Objectives
    Mission statement from annual reports
    Organizational structure
B. Service area staff perception of mission
    Adherence to stated goals
    Adherence to mission statement
C. Review of available research on service area
    Current student perceptions
    Community perceptions
    Prospective student perceptions

D. Service area wish lists
   Services needed but not provided
E. Analysis and recommendations
   Matching goals with results
   Matching wish lists with goals and results

In completing the self-studies, members of the task force were instructed to use one outline as a guide and to meet individually or in groups with staff members from each service area studied. It was felt that this would give a real picture of what services were being provided for students in each area.

The self-study reports produced several useful papers. In a survey of 1,330 currently enrolled spring 1985 students, it was found that 38.2 percent of the respondents already had an Associate of Arts degree and 16.1 percent already had a Bachelor of Arts degree or higher. The same survey also indicated that 77.6 percent of the students planned to pursue a bachelor's degree or beyond after the completion of their studies at the college. The survey also revealed that 61.2 percent of the respondents did not consider attending any other institution of higher education prior to their enrollment at the college. Of the 38.8 percent that considered attending other colleges, only large public four-year institutions were considered and no other community colleges were mentioned. It can be inferred from the results of the survey that the college is viewed as a viable higher education option.

Another worthwhile survey was the Career Student Follow-up Report completed in August 1985. This report surveyed all students who graduated from the college in any of its 19 career programs in 1983 or 1984. Overall, Johnson County Community College career students were pleased with the career program training they had received. Specifically they were pleased with the content of material covered in their career courses and the quality of instruction received. Career students were least satisfied with the college's counseling and placement services. Employers included in the Employer Follow-up portion of the survey rated the overall job preparation of the college's career students as excellent or good. Employers were especially impressed with the attitudes of the college's career students toward their work and their conceptual knowledge of various job functions.

A survey of 1,947 high school juniors and seniors enrolled in various Johnson County high schools indicated that Johnson County Community College and the University of Kansas were the two leading higher education alternatives considered for post high school attendance. Women respondents knew more about the college, held more favorable opinions toward the college, and were more likely to choose to attend the college than were male respondents. High school students who chose to attend the college tended to be less committed to their choice (Johnson County Community College) than students who chose to attend other colleges.

Finally, attitudes of parents in Johnson County were surveyed. A research report entitled Johnson County Parents' Educational and Career Aspirations for Their Eighth Grade Children indicated that the largest percentage of parents rated their children's attending a state four-year college or university in Kansas to be the most likely; a total of 57.2 percent of all responding parents indicated that their children would either definitely attend or probably attend such an institution. The local community college was the next most preferred institution among parents. Almost 31 percent of the respondents thought their children were likely to attend the local community college. In the section of the survey devoted to parents' career aspirations for their children, it was interesting to note that nearly half of all responding parents preferred either advanced degree professions such as lawyer, physician, or dentist, or technological professions such as engineer, computer programmer, or laboratory technician as the careers for their children. An overwhelming majority of parents surveyed hoped that their children pursued white collar careers and only 3.7 percent indicated any interest in trade and craft, traditionally blue collar careers.

Analysis of the research by the task force led to the belief that the college was viewed in a positive light by community members, and was well respected. These reports and other self-study documents led the committee to conclude that Johnson County Community College was in a strong position to recruit and retain local students. The objective became, therefore, to capitalize on these strengths to build a sound, ongoing approach to student recruitment and retention.

In reviewing the reports, it was obvious that all areas of the college were genuinely concerned about student recruitment and customer satisfaction. One item that frequently appeared on the wish list was a need for better campus-wide communication and staff training regarding enrollment management issues. Just by virtue of the numbers of people employed by the college, communication became vitally important.

Many recommendations focused on a lack of training for faculty and staff in the area of policy and procedure relating to the admissions and enrollment of students. Examples sighted by the admissions and records staff included incorrect information given to students by faculty and academic division offices on enrollment procedures, refund policies, and graduation requirements.

Other specific concerns also related to information given to students. The counseling staff recommended mandatory counseling for all students but recognized that this could not occur without the assistance of faculty program coordinators. Other concerns were the quality of counseling services given in relationship to counselor/student ratio, lack of soundproof confidential offices, and overcrowded conditions in the counseling center.

An overall theme that permeated the reports was a need for enhanced coordination and cooperation among areas of the college related to the recruitment of students. As an example, the dean of students edited and produced the college catalog, the associate dean of continuing education produced the credit and noncredit course bulletins, the director of public information produced the college view book, and the dean of students produced the college career brochures. Centralized coordination of these publications would allow their uniformity, permit more effective targeting of marketing activities, and at the same time eliminate the duplication of effort and provide for increased efficiency.

Student retention became a primary focus when the office of institutional research noted the importance of the bond between the student and the college in student retention. The office of institutional research indicated that the faculty was the most important component in establishing this bond. Student surveys continually pointed to the strength of the teaching faculty as being the main reason students attend the college and why they would recommend attendance to other potential students. The college needed to capitalize on the faculty for retention purposes and train them to ensure consistently high quality in all classes. A new faculty evaluation process by students, implemented in the spring 1985 term, was a step in the right direction for improving teaching effectiveness, but there remained a need to communicate student service policies and procedures throughout the college.

ORGANIZATIONAL OVERVIEW AS IT RELATES TO THE NEEDS OF ENROLLMENT MANAGEMENT

As with most community colleges, most of the responsibility for student admissions was located within the student services area at Johnson County Community College. As the organization chart in Table 4.1 indicates, the chief administrator of the student services area is the dean of student services. The dean reports to the vice-president of academic affairs who, in turn, reports to the president of the college.

Within the student services area, various directors administer the different functional areas. The director of admissions, records, and financial aid manages the enrollment, financial aid, and registration functions. The director of counseling and student development manages student advisement and counseling, career planning and placement, and testing and assessment.

Table 4.1. Organization Chart, Student Services

Dean of Student Services				
Director of Student Activities	Director of Admissions, Records, and Financial Aid	Director of Auxiliary Services	Director of Special Services	Director of Student Development and Counseling
Program Adviser	Financial Aid Officer	Vending Supervisor	Special Services	Coordinator, Testing and Assessment Center
Housing and Program Assistant	Admissions and Records Officer	Child Play Center Manager	Gallaudet Center	
		Bookstore Manager	Career Exploration	
		Food Service Manager	Interpreter Training Program	

The director of auxiliary services manages the food service, bookstore, and child play center. The director of student activities manages all student organizations and activities including student government and entertainment functions. And finally, the director of special services manages handicapped services, including a program for a large population of hearing-impaired students.

The student services area of the college is part of academic affairs and both the dean of students and academic dean report directly to the academic vice president. To capitalize on the advantages this type of organizational structure provides for a solid enrollment management concept that allows a high degree of faculty and administrative involvement, a cohesive effort needed to be undertaken.

RECOMMENDATIONS

As with any new concept, change needed to be made gradually and with the cooperation of everyone involved. For the short term, the recommended approach would be to build on the existing organization using the matrix approach to enrollment management, as described by Kemerer, Baldridge, and Green (1982). The matrix approach would require that the academic vice president act as the standing chair of the Enrollment Management Advisory Council. This would instill the administrative commitment to enrollment management on all those involved in the student recruitment efforts of the college. The admission of students would be maintained under the director of admissions, records, and financial aid, who would still report to the dean of students. The only organizational changes required would be a realignment of responsibilities, with the areas of recruitment, publications, and admissions counseling services placed under the direct supervision of the director of admissions, records, and financial aid. In addition, the director would be given input into the research agenda of the college and work directly with the office of institutional research in creating an enrollment master plan based on community perceptions of the college and significant demographic trends.

The matrix approach would be designed to fit into the organizational structure of the college, as outlined in Figure 4.1. An integral part of the approach would be the preservation of the Enrollment Management Advisory Council reporting directly to the president. The intent of this would be to keep enrollment management at the forefront of emphasis by the college.

The enrollment management area housed in the organizational structure in student services would be linked to the faculty and support services areas of the college through the Enrollment Management Advisory Council. A key component of the entire structure would be the role of staff development and training. A training agenda would be developed by the Enrollment Management Advisory Council and would be carried out by the staff development office of the college. Specific emphasis would be on student-oriented services with the goal of having uniform knowledge in all offices of the college related to student needs.

The most important link in the entire enrollment management concept of Johnson County Community College would be the role of the faculty. The research we did indicated that students were very pleased with the quality of the faculty and the instruction received. In light of this, the college needed to capitalize on the strength of the faculty.

To strengthen the bond between the students and the faculty, a training program would be designed through the Enrollment Management Advisory Council by faculty, for faculty. The purpose of the program would be to emphasize classroom services and teaching effectiveness by using the master teacher concept (explained later). The program would be tailored to individual departments by key faculty members within the unit and participation would be voluntary for faculty members. Faculty members of the Enrollment Management Advisory Council would be given released time to research and design the best possible program for their department. During the design phase, routine updates would be provided for all faculty and suggestions for modification and improvement would be encouraged.

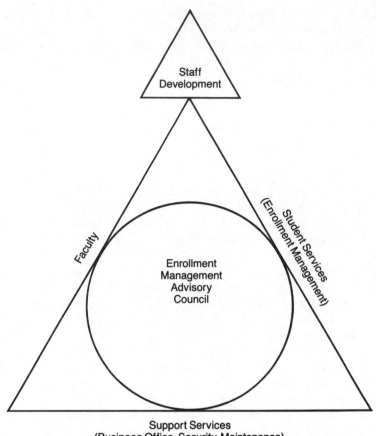

Figure 4.1. Enrollment Management Matrix.

Once a program was developed for a department, it would be tested in a classroom situation by several faculty members and adjustments and modifications would be made for the final plan.

Components of the plan would include the following:

- Uniform format for all course outlines and abstracts
- General outline for first class meeting lecture covering student service areas including:
    Tutoring
    Graduation requirements
    Class withdrawal procedures
    Refund procedures

- Faculty intervention for nonperformers including:
  Telephone calls to nonattending students
  Required meetings with students experiencing academic difficulty

In addition, master teachers would visit the classrooms of participating instructors to observe classroom techniques. Advice would be given on areas for improvement with a plan of action for self-improvement.

The key to the program is that it would be managed entirely by the faculty for improvement of teaching effectiveness. The goal would be to provide a system for teaching improvement in the least threatening environment possible. This would be accomplished in a faculty-managed program and would not be possible in something managed or mandated by the administration of the college. Generally, faculty members are more trusting of colleagues in the same teaching discipline or department than of anyone else in that organization.

By embracing the concept of the master teacher, which not only addresses teaching effectiveness but also student involvement, the attractiveness of the college to potential and current students can be enhanced. Better classroom service by the faculty members would increase the bond between the student and the college and would contribute to the retention and continued enrollment for succeeding semesters by students.

CRITIQUE

The most difficult task in implementing an enrollment management concept at Johnson County Community College has been overcoming the various political obstacles. As in any organization, staff members were concerned with losing their power base, or, conversely, being assigned additional duties they did not have time for. As stated earlier, developing our enrollment management committee was proposed in order to overcome the perceived problems of incorporating an enrollment management concept into the existing structure in the student services area.

In retrospect, appointing the vice president for academic affairs as chairman of the task force may have been more prudent. A higher ranking administrator as chairman would have better demonstrated the importance of the task force and may have eliminated some of the behind the scenes maneuvering. Additionally, the involvement of a person at that level may have demonstrated the administration's commitment to such a degree as to encourage even greater motivation and interest on the part of task force members.

The chances for a successful enrollment management concept on the Johnson County Community College campus are very high. The entire year-long process of studying what the college is doing to attract and retain students served to emphasize the importance of working together among the various departments of the college. By having some key people participate in the project, lines of communication were established that did not exist in the past. The process renewed a commitment to doing whatever was required to help the college achieve its enrollment goals. Several items resulted from the work of the task force, including:

- Revised advertising philosophy placing emphasis on faculty, staff, and student testimonials.
- Carry-over emphasis from print ads to radio ads using some of the same people.
- Telephone campaign to early registrants who did not pay tuition by the required invoice date.
- Organized training program for hourly support personnel educating them on all student service areas.

Most of the ideas were the result of the input of faculty and staff involved in the task force. In reviewing the various self-studies that were completed, an outline was used that analyzed each problem along the following dimensions: problem, causes, effects, and solution(s). The reports were reviewed by the task force as a whole and the collective wisdom of the task force resulted in some very creative solutions to identified problems. This became a foundation for future enrollment management activities at Johnson County Community College. A standing task force, composed of faculty, staff, and administrators, maintaining high levels of communication, discussing enrollment concerns in a logical problem solving mode, and coming up with solutions based on a consensus of the group was recommended.

The future of enrollment management at Johnson County Community College, as with the inception of the entire project, rests with the president. At Johnson County Community College, like anywhere else, the final implementation of a new philosophy and its resulting acceptance will depend on its initial presentation and perceived administrative support. Because that commitment is present at Johnson County Community College, we can say, again, that the chances for an effective enrollment management plan are very high.

Commentary by Don Hossler

Of the four case studies in this book, the efforts of Johnson Country Community College have the most recent beginnings. Their systematic enrollment management activities began only in 1984. The effectiveness of their efforts cannot yet be determined. Nevertheless, the Johnson County case study helps to illustrate several issues that have been discussed in the first three chapters.

The experience of Johnson County Community College is a clear example of rational change. In this case, the president facilitated the change process when he became interested in enrollment management. The president sought more information from the director of admissions, records, and financial aid and subsequently decided that he wanted to implement an enrollment management plan at his institution. Thus, as the rational change model posits, there was support from at least one senior level administrator. The director of admissions, records, and financial aid was the "idea champion" at Johnson County.

A threat to the institution, in the form of a projected credit hour shortfall, became visible on the horizon. As the time line for the rational change model suggests, the threat was not a major one at that point, but it was important. Also in keeping with the rational change model, the organization was a stable one so that no dramatic actions seemed necessary. These conditions created a situation that was ripe for the utilization of a planned change model. There was no major environmental threat on the horizon, so rapid change was neither necessary nor desirable. A potential solution was present in the form of the enrollment management concept, and a senior level administrator was an advocate of the change process.

The type of system that has emerged at Johnson County Community College is also consistent with rational change. Johnson County started with an enrollment management committee. The committee played two important roles. First the committee was charged with making a set of recommendations. These recommendations led to the creation of a matrix system. Perhaps equally important, the committee served an educative role in that key administrators, staff, and faculty began to understand the factors related to enrollments. These committee members in turn have the opportunity to become advocates for the enrollment management concept. The evolutionary nature of the four enrollment management models is also evident from this case study. Johnson County began with a committee. From the committee a coordinator was appointed. Even in the time since Will Chatham wrote his case study, the system at Johnson County has continued to evolve. A matrix system is now in place, the academic vice-president coordinates the matrix model.

It is also interesting to note the emphasis of the enrollment management activities at Johnson County Community College. The imagery of coupling is helpful in understanding what has been happening at Johnson County. In the area of recruitment and admissions, the college has more "tightly

coupled" its publications and marketing efforts. Clarifying enrollment procedures, providing more accurate information to prospective students, and
giving more attention to the actual recruitment of students can also be
viewed as paying more attention to the linkages in these areas. Student
retention activities have centered around efforts to increase the quality of
instruction and the quality of student–faculty interaction. In this chapter,
Will Chatham uses the term "bonding" to describe institutional retention
efforts. The similarities between terms like coupling and bonding are apparent. The continuance of the enrollment management committee as part
of the matrix system suggests that the campus will continue to more closely
"couple" enrollment management issues.

The final point that requires emphasis in this case study is the variety
and complexity of activities that Johnson County Community College has
engaged in during the time it has been developing an enrollment management plan. So many attempts to engage in enrollment management end up
focusing exclusively on marketing and recruitment. This is certainly a
component of the Johnson County efforts, but institutional efforts go
beyond this narrow set of activities. At Johnson County they are looking
at student retention, and have surveyed potential students, parents, and
the general community. The information they gathered on the satisfaction
of their graduates with career preparation, on employer satisfaction with
Johnson County graduates, and the success of their transfer students at
four-year colleges and universities is part of the outcomes lens of an
enrollment management system. This demonstrates that institutional administrators appreciate the complex factors that influence student enrollments.

The importance of information, and hence management science, in shaping the plans of the committee is evident throughout the chapter. The case
study also discusses the role of academic experiences in improving retention. This is quite consistent with some of the findings of Pascarella and
colleagues (Pascarella and Terenzini 1980; Pascarella et al. 1981). They
note that academic integration, rather than social integration, is more
strongly related to student persistence on commuter campuses. Although
the case study does not mention it explicitly, quality academic programs
also play a very important role in attracting students. Johnson County
Community College's emphasis on improving the quality of the classroom
experience should have many positive benefits for them.

Is there anything that seems to be overlooked in the efforts of Johnson
County Community College? No mention is made of the role of financial
aid or tuition in their enrollment management efforts. Therefore it is not
clear whether the institution has evidence to suggest that this has no
significant bearing on enrollments, or whether they have not yet turned

their attention to this issue. Since financial aid is part of admissions and records, the campus is in a good position to coordinate all of these activities as part of its courtship plan.

The case study mentions that alumni were dissatisfied with career placement assistance. Assisting graduates in finding jobs is an element of an enrollment management system that should not be overlooked. There is no discussion of what steps the institution is taking in this area. No mention is made of academic assistance programs. These too should not be overlooked, particularly at a community college where there are likely to be more poorly prepared students.

Overall, it appears that Johnson County Community College is off to a good start in its efforts to implement an enrollment management system. Since the enrollment management plan is just starting, its effectiveness cannot yet be evaluated. The evaluation component, however, should become an ongoing part of the institution's enrollment management activities. The Johnson County Community College case study is potentially useful for many institutions. On most campuses where senior level administrators attempt to intentionally develop an enrollment management plan, they are likely to follow steps very similar to those used at Johnson County Community College.

Chapter 5

A Case Study: DePaul University

Patricia Ewers

During the decade from 1970 to 1980, DePaul University, a private, multipurpose institution located in Chicago, Illinois, benefited from increases in enrollments in nearly all of its colleges and schools. After reaching a university high of 13,356 students in 1980–81, DePaul faced a major decline in its undergraduate population. The university's response was to organize, plan, and implement an enrollment management program to ensure the institution's future and to maintain an annual balanced operating budget in the interval. What follows is a description of the institutional circumstances, the responses to them, and some reflections on the cost of these changes and on the lessons learned.

DePaul University shares characteristics with many of the universities that describe themselves as urban and Catholic and that have undergone the change from simple to increasingly complex institutions. Founded by the Vincentian fathers in 1898, DePaul moved from a small college that offered a limited curriculum for a youthful student population to multiple schools and colleges that offer a wide variety of academic and professional programs to large, diverse student populations. At present, the university has eight colleges and schools: The College of Liberal Arts and Sciences, the College of Commerce, the School of Accountancy, the College of Law, the School of Music, the School of Education, the School for New Learning, an innovative college for adults, and the Theatre School founded as The Goodman School of Drama in 1925.

The special circumstances of urban institutions have required that more than organizational and curricular changes take place. DePaul University has accepted the responsibility for serving student populations whose num-

PATRICIA EWERS has been vice president/dean of faculties at DePaul University for six years.

bers and diversity of sex, creed, age, and ethnic background have increased as social and economic changes have made higher education both desirable and possible for them. As an essential obligation, DePaul has offered services to this broader clientele by developing strategies to make its programs available to the people whom it wishes to serve. Among the most common are the use of financial aid to assist the students in meeting the growing costs of private education; multiple locations to accommodate commuting students; the scheduling of programs during the summer, at night, and on weekends for the convenience of students who are employed full-time; and special counseling and orientation services. Thus DePaul is a university that operates year-round, day and night, including the weekends, on three campuses: a campus in the heart of the Chicago commercial center, a campus on the near north side located in an exceptionally fine residential area, and a campus in the northwest suburbs near the O'Hare Airport.

DePaul's students come predominantly from metropolitan Chicago. Although in recent years there has been increasing demand from beyond the urban area, latest figures still indicate that more than 90 percent of DePaul's students are recruited from the City of Chicago and its suburban communities. Most students work, and just under half attend evening or weekend programs. Of the present 7,800 who are undergraduates, more than 40 percent are nontraditional students aged 24 or older. In addition, DePaul serves 5,200 graduate and professional students, including doctoral students in the Ph.D. programs in psychology and philosophy. Admission to all programs is on a "selective" or "highly selective" basis.

Financially, DePaul has a modest endowment of 18 million dollars, a history of balanced, frugal budgets, and serious dependency on tuition for nearly 90 percent of its revenue. The majority of dollars, which have been raised through gifts and grants, have been used to build the endowment, to fund the development of the physical plant, and to develop and to support academic programs.

After years of constantly increasing enrollments, which peaked in 1980–81, the long-predicted decline of traditional-aged students finally hit DePaul University. The relative stability of the graduate enrollment and a planned decrease in the population of the College of Law completed the total picture. From fall 1980 to fall 1983, the head count dropped from 13,356 to 12,447 (−6.9 percent) (see Table 5.1) and, more important, the credit hours, the measure of revenue generation, dropped from 138,764 to 122,728 (−11.56 percent).

An analysis of the sources of new freshmen and transfers during this period pinpointed the problem and revealed that the record enrollments of 1980–81 had masked the beginning of a decline in the undergraduate

Table 5.1. Headcount Enrollment by Level, Fall 1979 to Fall 1983

	1979	1980	1981	1982	1983
Undergraduate	8,101	8,455	8,330	7,911	7,694
% Change	4.9	4.4	−1.5	−5.0	−2.7
Graduate	3,476	3,596	3,697	3,739	3,606
% Change	8.5	3.5	2.8	1.1	−3.6
Professional	1,280	1,305	1,273	1,217	1,147
% Change	4.8	2.0	−2.5	−4.4	−5.8
Total	12,857	13,356	13,300	12,867	12,447
% Change	5.8	3.9	−0.4	−3.3	−3.3

Table 5.2. Applications, Acceptances, and Enrollment Trends for Under-graduates, Fall 1979 to Fall 1983

	1979	1980	1981	1982	1983
First-Time Freshmen					
No. of Applications	2,238	2,579	2,381	1,862	1,864
% Annual Change	−3.58	15.24	−7.68	−21.80	0.11
No. of Acceptances	1,497	1,538	1,406	1,385	1,227
% Annual Change	37.59	2.74	−8.58	−1.49	−11.41
No. of Enrollments	1,020	946	799	691	653
% Annual Change	0.49	−7.25	−15.54	−13.52	−5.50
Transfers					
No. of Applications	1,351	1,779	1,511	1,224	1,381
% Annual Change	−3.98	31.68	−15.06	−18.99	12.83
No. of Acceptances	1,056	1,074	887	992	956
% Annual Change	26.32	1.70	−17.41	11.84	−3.63
No. of Enrollments	822	681	589	636	653
% Annual Change	10.19	−17.15	−13.51	7.98	2.67

population. From fall 1979 to fall 1983, enrolled freshmen dropped from 1,020 to 653 (−35.98 percent) and transfer students from 822 to 589 (−28.3 percent) in 1981 with a small recovery to 653 (+10.86 percent) by 1983. The decline in enrolled students (Table 5.2) was a direct result of the decline in the number of applications received and in the total numbers accepted by the institution.

There were three major causes of these declines in applications: the decline in the traditional-aged population; the practices of the offices of admission and financial aid; and the growing selectivity of the university. During this period the number of high school graduates in the state of Illinois declined by approximately 14,000, certainly a contributing factor to the institution's situation. But an analysis of the university's market share of first-time freshmen indicated that in Cook County, the primary market of DePaul, the university had dropped from a 10.8 to an 8.1 percent share and in the state of Illinois as a whole, the market share dropped from 6.3 to 4.3 percent.

Thus the university had to face the reality that its program of recruitment was not as effective as that of its competitors. Because the preceding decade of growth had strained the resources of the office of admission, it cut back on its high school and community college visits and contacts in an effort to make timely responses to the growing number of applications and the requests by interested prospects for appointments and counseling. The office of financial aid, lacking the appropriate computer support, struggled to make awards according to federal and state guidelines but never utilized aid as a strategic element in attracting or enrolling students. While the university had not increased resources for either of these offices beyond incremental appropriations for a number of years, the university, as a whole, looked solely to them for solutions to its enrollment problems, as long as the results did not diminish the institutional quality.

In fact, some of the decline was probably the result of university actions taken in the late 1970s to strengthen its academic programs. For example, in the College of Commerce, the admission requirements were raised for transfer students to require a grade-point average of 3.0 on a 4.0-point scale. The liberal studies program, the general education requirements for all undergraduate students, was strengthened by increases in the number of courses required and in the difficulty of the courses. Finally, the university introduced placement testing in mathematics, writing, and reading for all incoming students. Required levels of competence had to be demonstrated through test scores or performance in courses. These changes resulted in the loss of the least qualified third of the applicant pool during the critical five-year period.

The situation at DePaul demanded immediate and effective action to end the dramatic decreases in students and to avoid a major budgetary crisis. The long-term response had to be a change from a recruitment effort isolated in the office of admission to an enrollment management program. The former characterized recruitment strategies based on cultivating the widest possible pool of prospects who were later evaluated in the light of institutional criteria. The latter depends on the identification of the number and characteristics of the desired students for each of the academic units, the analysis of the marketplace to discover the sources of those specific students, and the design and implementation of strategies for recruiting and retaining the targeted goals. The former was more passive and responsive to external circumstances; the latter is active and attempts to manipulate the external circumstances in the light of internal priorities.

Enrollment management was to be more than a temporary response to the need of the institution to counter the adverse enrollment figures of four years. Simply stated, the purpose of the program was to grant the institution the freedom to determine its own future and to gain control of its destiny by careful planning to find, to recruit, and to retain the students it chose to enroll in its academic programs.

Because the university's environment had changed from an expanding institution in which resources were growing more plentiful to one in which the decline in the tuition revenue was beginning to restrict severely the operating budget, the determined, effective, and efficient marketing of academic programs was no longer a choice but a necessity. The question was not whether marketing strategies were necessary, but whether they were to be the product of a process that reflected the academic goals and mission of the university.

Since the circumstances under which this enrollment management plan was to be introduced were less than ideal, they demanded immediate interventions and short-term results in order for the institution to survive with quality until long-term strategies could take effect. The administration was constantly aware of the tension between immediate needs and long-term concerns and was challenged to make decisions that produced positive results for both.

The fundamental questions posed by the need to manage enrollments for both the present and the future were the same: What is the mission of the institution? What does it wish to become? The first step in the process of transition was the incorporation of the issues related to enrollments into the deliberations on these strategic questions.

Enrollment management, then, was to become an instrument or aspect of academic planning and would only be considered in the context of the broader policies, goals, and educational mission of the university. Removed from the context, the effort to control enrollments would become merely adventitious, the product of loosely connected marketing strategies unrelated to the present or anticipated needs of the institution.

The second major step in the process was to produce the essential research needed by the administration for the development and evaluation of the recruitment goals and marketing strategies. The office of planning and institutional research provided statistics on the numbers, quality, socioeconomic and geographical backgrounds of the student population at DePaul. The office also analyzed market-share information and developed data for the university to determine its institutional position in relation to its competition. The result was a far better understanding of the opportunities for attracting the quantity, distribution, and quality of students desired.

While efforts in planning and research were preparing the institution to address the longer-term issues, the administration had to address the immediate problem of declining enrollments if it wished to reduce budgetary pressures. Between fall 1982 and spring 1983, the university took some initial steps.

1. Upon the retirement of the director of admission, the university hired an administrator who introduced the concepts of enrollment management and who convinced the vice president/dean of faculties of the need to assume personal leadership in designing the model and developing institutional support.
2. The deans of the colleges and schools accepted the responsibility for setting enrollment goals for their units.
3. Some effort was made to make financial aid a part of the recruitment strategy.
4. There was a growing awareness of the need for timeliness in university actions in order to achieve successful recruiting.
5. There were initial conversations in other areas of the university about the need for them to serve as part of the delivery system for recruitment and retention programs.
6. There was agreement on a strategy for fall 1983, which emphasized (1) an increase in the yield from the pool of accepted freshmen, since their numbers were considerably reduced, and (2) special efforts to increase the transfer population in order to slow the overall rate of decline.

Most of these changes, however, occurred as uncoordinated pieces. There was still a need for a coherent and coordinated design that addressed the goals, the administrative structures, the calendar, and the institutional commitment necessary for the implementation of the program in time to influence recruitment for the class of 1984. The vice president/dean of faculties prepared a working paper during March 1983 that raised the central institutional issues and proposed a plan for the future. This document then became the basis of discussion at the various administrative levels. The university community was made a part of the discussion through a number of open forums to which administrators, faculty, and staff were invited for presentations by the vice president/dean of faculties and the director of admission. They described the enrollment situation, identified the new model, responded to questions, and accepted valuable constructive criticism. In the minds of many members of the university, these sessions were crucial to creating the commitment of the faculty and staff to the success of this enterprise.

The planning document called for the establishment of goals for the number, quality, and characteristics of the desired and appropriate students for each academic area; an assignment of responsibilities related to enrollment management to the key decision makers; a reorganization of the calendar to coordinate better with the cycles of prospects' decisions; and a university-wide commitment to the program. Throughout the document, there were two principal themes: first, that enrollment management was a means of fulfilling institutional goals and plans rather than a substitute for them; second, that effective recruitment and retention depended on a mutual selection process involving the prospects and the institution. The university was to be a partner in a search for the right match between the academic needs of the students and the programs of the university.

Spring 1983 became the critical turning point in the institutional situation because the enrollment management plan was introduced. During that period, the colleges and schools worked on their planning documents and addressed the relationship of the appropriate student population to their academic goals and programs. In the early phases the two major concerns were numbers and academic quality. More recent planning has become more specific in describing student mix for particular programs and has begun to focus on issues related to age, minorities, geographic origins, and socioeconomic status. These goals were and are evaluated in the light of the institutional mission as well as their financial implications.

Since the effectiveness of a program of recruitment and retention strategies was totally dependent on key decisions made in a timely fashion and implemented by the appropriate offices, the university, at first, considered creating a special administrative structure to manage and to coordinate the programs. Careful analysis indicated that such a change would only add a cumbersome layer between those individuals who must make the decisions and those who must implement them. Indeed, an earlier reorganization in 1981 of the key administrative areas of the office of admission, the financial aid office, and the assessment and advisement center under a dean who reported directly to the academic vice president provided an excellent model of organization for the coordination of academic and administrative activities. The vice president/dean of faculties had only to clarify and to assign responsibilities within that administrative structure.

One major change, however, was necessary. The position of dean for undergraduate assessment and admission had originally been conceived as primarily academic in nature. The need for far more aggressive recruitment led to the resignation of the dean in spring 1983 and the creation of a new position, an associate vice president for enrollment management. The vice president/dean of faculties took immediate supervisory responsibility for the area pending the hiring of the new person, who would have extensive experience in enrollment management.

The assignment of responsibilities within the university's administrative structure was designed to provide coordination of the university's actions with the decision calendar of the prospective students.

Basically, there are two timetables or decision-making processes that are interdependent: that of the prospective student and that of the institution. The student first decides to investigate a number of institutions, then applies to a selected few, and, finally, enrolls at one institution. At each of these crucial points, information from and intervention by the institution can positively influence the student. Thus there must be activities directed at each of these decision points. Recruitment is the active identification and cultivation of a student through the application process. Yield activities are directed at those students who have applied and been accepted but must still be provided with continuing positive experiences of the institution so that the final choice from among multiple applications results in enrollment. Retention activities target the continuing student whose actual experiences of the educational offerings and support services form the basis for a decision to remain or to leave. Figure 5.1 shows the institution's organizational response to these needs.

With regard to the responsibilities for timely decisions and actions, members of the Administrative Council decided on the assignment of key responsibilities, provided the funds to the offices that executed the activity, gave final approval to the enrollment goals and marketing plan, and enforced calendar deadlines for key decisions. Once the Administrative Council assigned the key responsibilities and approved the necessary budgetary allocations, the process of designing the plan for a specific year began 18 months in advance of the enrollment of a specific group of students. For example, in spring 1983, the institution began planning for the enrollments for fall 1984.

The coordination of this planning, the creation of a context within which the deans set enrollment goals, and the development of marketing strategies were the assigned responsibility of the newly created office of the associate vice president for enrollment management. Because this position remained unfilled until fall 1984, the coordinating role was filled by the vice president/dean of faculties during the implementation of the program. While this additional responsibility had some negative consequences for the total effectiveness of that office, there is no doubt that the direct involvement of the highest ranking academic officer in the university was a major signal to the community of the importance of the enterprise.

The college deans, in consultation with individual departments, set the specific enrollment goals for their areas. Since enrollments could not be effectively managed without tying recruitment goals to long-term academic goals of the individual units, recruitment goals did not originate with the office of admission. On the other hand, the recruitment goals of individual academic units had to be coordinated with each other and with the larger purposes and mission of the university. Therefore, the Deans' Council and the vice president/dean of faculties, in consultation with the Administrative

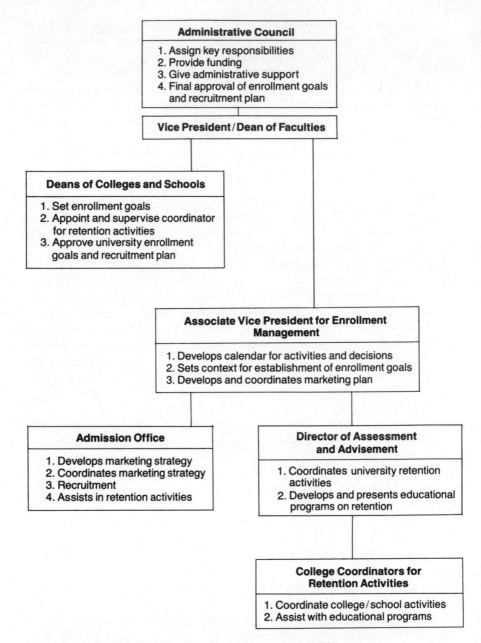

Figure 5.1. Organization for Enrollment Management Plan.

Council, were responsible for agreeing upon and informing the office of admission of the enrollment and recruitment priorities of the university. The director of admission worked with individual deparment chairmen and college deans within the priorities established by that council.

To describe adequately the further division of responsibility for the implementation of the program, it is necessary to recall the need for both recruitment and yield activities. The office of admission was primarily responsible for the recruitment of new students. While that office re-quested the support of the academic areas in its activities, it concentrated on identifying markets, contacting appropriate students, providing them with necessary information, and shepherding them through the application process.

After students were accepted, the responsibilities were shared by the college/school/department offices so that a more personal and continuing contact could be made with every student. Each dean appointed a specific person within the college to coordinate that area's efforts and to act as a liaison with the admission office. The dean also "sold" involvement to his or her faculty and sponsored educational programs on enrollment issues for faculty and staff.

Centralizing the yield activities within the colleges and schools helped the university avoid the situation that most institutions faced: the myriad and competing requests for information and assistance that were all directed to the admission office. Instead, the admission office served the academic area as the source of an overall strategy, assisted in developing the educa-tional programs for the academic units, and participated in specific activities or events whenever possible.

In addition, the director of the assessment and advisement center was appointed the university coordinator for retention of continuing students. He was primarily responsible for the coordination of retention activities throughout the university, for offering educational programs on retention strategies, and for the annual evaluation of the effectiveness of these activ-ities. The university has had little success, thus far, in implementing this part of the program. The lack of success has been the result of a primary focus on the recruitment of new students, an inappropriate assignment of responsibility at an institutional level that could not be effective, and a lack of sufficient and appropriate data. The responsibility for retention has now been reassigned to the associate vice president for enrollment management.

The administration accomplished these changes with a minimum of ter-ritorial conflict. While there were arguments over minor items such as which office would pay for the refreshments at an open house or the postage for recruitment mailings, the disputes were settled quickly and no lingering hostilities developed. The environment of crisis and the need for cooperation to achieve institutional goals took precedence over the smaller issues.

The development of enrollment goals, the assignment of key responsibilities, the achievement of timely decisions, and the institutional commitment of resources to the program were the key elements in addressing both the immediate and the long-range issues related to improving DePaul's enrollments. There were a number of other actions that the university took to ensure success. First, there was a reallocation of institutional resources so that the staff and resources of the office of admission could be expanded to meet the new demands and the university publications could be reevaluated and redone to fit the agreed-upon institutional image. Second, the university substantially upgraded the support for enrollment management by the administrative computer and the office of planning and institutional research. Both were necessary in order to develop an ongoing research component that included a demographic analysis of key market areas, an admitted and no-show study, and an analysis of the effectiveness of financial aid strategies. Finally, the university established an atmosphere in which risk taking was encouraged and mistakes used as learning experiences. The consequences were seen in an increase in creativity, an enthusiasm for the enterprise, and a strong sense of comradeship.

The results of the first full year of the program were dramatic (Table 5.3). The small successes of 1983, in which the rate of decline in new freshmen was reduced to −5.5 percent and transfer students were increased by 2.67 percent, was dwarfed by the result of 1984. In that year freshmen increased by 15.31 percent and transfer students by 20.67 percent. These numbers were achieved without any reduction in admission requirements or in the overall quality of the incoming class as demonstrated by ACT and SAT profiles. The enrollments in 1985 were also gratifying. During both years, the increase in enrollments followed directly from increases in applications and acceptances.

The increases in the undergraduate population were not reflected immediately in positive figures in total university enrollments because of the presence of the smaller classes of 1982 and 1983, which were migrating through the system. However, a 4.14 percent increase in the total figures in fall 1985 (Table 5.4) demonstrates the effectiveness of the enrollment management program at DePaul.

For the future, the university intends to maintain its enrollments at their current levels except for a few undergraduate programs that have underutilized capacity. This goal is not a minor one since the decline in traditional-aged students will continue in Illinois until 1992 and the competition for students of the quality DePaul wishes to attract will grow more and more fierce. The presence of the newly appointed associate vice president

Table 5.3. Applications, Acceptances, and Enrollment Trends for Under-graduates, Fall 1983 to Fall 1985

	1983	1984	1985
First-Time Freshmen			
No. of Applications	1,864	2,133	2,482
% Annual Change	0.11	14.43	16.36
No. of Acceptances	1,227	1,523	1,709
% Annual Change	−11.41	24.12	12.21
No. of Enrollments	653	753	838
% Annual Change	−5.50	15.31	11.28
Transfers			
No. of Applications	1,381	1,387	1,800
% Annual Change	12.83	0.43	29.77
No. of Acceptances	956	1,173	1,381
% Annual Change	−3.63	22.70	17.73
No. of Enrollments	653	788	875
% Annual Change	2.67	20.67	11.04

Table. 5.4. Headcount Enrollment by Level, Fall 1983 to Fall 1985

	1983	1984	1985
Undergraduate	7,694	7,379	7,714
% Change	−2.7	−4.1	+4.54
Graduate	3,606	3,821	4,052
% Change	−3.6	+6.0	+6.05
Professional	1,147	1,126	1,070
% Change	−5.8	−1.8	−4.97
Total	12,447	12,326	12,836
% Change	−3.3	−1.0	+4.14

for enrollment management has provided the university with an administrator with extensive experience in leading enrollment programs and in translating institutional goals into recruitment strategies. Through her leadership, institutional attention is presently focused upon clarification of the university's strategic positioning as the basis of its marketing approach and improvement of the printed materials that represent the university. In addition, she will provide the needed leadership to strengthen retention efforts within the university.

In describing the university's experience, the author has placed particular emphasis upon planning, research, institutional organization and commitment, and timeliness of activities rather than on tactics used to recruit students. That emphasis arises from a fundamental belief that DePaul's success in such a brief period of time was due to the ability of the institution as a whole to respond to a crisis situation with a coordinated effort from all levels and to utilize the enrollment management program as a means of furthering institutional goals.

These achievements were not accomplished without costs. Such a dramatic turnaround demanded enormous commitments of time and energy. It also demanded flexibility and balance in the face of constantly changing circumstances. DePaul paid the price in the loss of good people, financial resources, opportunities, and institutional innocence.

Many good people who had served the university well for years found that the accelerating rate of change and the uncertainty arising from it produced an environment that for them was counterproductive. The result was that DePaul lost some loyal employees. For example, in the critical five-year period, there were three directors of admission; in the short span, the director of financial aid reported to five different individuals and, finally, left the institution in frustration.

Not all those who left chose to go. There were a number of individuals who could not adapt to the changing circumstances or develop a new set of skills and were asked to leave. These departures also exacted an institutional cost in the search for replacements and the orientation of new employees.

During the critical two-year turnaround period, DePaul made some mistakes and, probably, spent too much money. In terms of the overall stakes, these errors and costs were neither frequent nor high. If the university had addressed the issues prior to the onset of declines in enrollments, then a more thorough analysis of the probabilities of success or of the total costs could have been calculated. Given an emergency situation, the administration took the position that inaction was the greater risk.

The university will never be able to assess fully the costs of lost opportunities that slipped away while the energy and attention of key administrators were focused on building enrollments. The vice president/dean of faculties, the academic deans, and the university budget committee were preoccupied with this issue to the detriment of program development and evaluation. At present, it appears that no serious or sustained problems have resulted, but the opportunities for other positive accomplishments in that time period are lost.

The final cost to the university and, perhaps, to all of higher education in America today is an institutional loss of innocence. It is disturbing to the values of educators when their work is dependent on maintaining market share, finding the right institutional image or position, and developing successful tuition/discount models. Faculty members and academic administrators no longer have the privilege of believing in institutional survival based on the quality of the enterprise. Fine institutions are struggling today, many because they have refused to understand that higher education is now in a buyer's market with the future of age-old values often resting in the untried hands of 18-year-old potential students. Since the academic world is no longer the sole evaluator of its effectiveness, universities must recognize that the perception of those served may not be the same as the institution's. As a consequence, higher education has lost its innocence and cannot disregard the judgments of potential clientele, the state of the economy of the nation, or the strategies of the marketplace.

While one can look with nostalgia at the passing of the "golden age" of growth in higher education, the future, with its set of challenges, may ultimately prove more rewarding. Every institution will have the opportunity to take a hard look at its reasons for existence and the quality of its instructional and research activities. If an institution wants to meet the challenges of this far more competitive situation, it will find that enrollment management is an invaluable and essential element for controlling that future.

In evaluating and planning for the use of an enrollment management model, the university administrator should be aware of the essentials of a successful program.

1. Enrollment management is a means of achieving institutional goals and planning rather than a substitute for them.
2. Effective enrollment management and marketing strategy must arise out of research and subject the program to thorough evaluation.
3. At the heart of all successful marketing is the ability of the institution to treat the prospective student as an individual whom it is assisting in finding the right match.
4. The university that introduces an enrollment management program in crisis circumstances must be willing to pay the costs in people, dollars, energy, and lost opportunities.
5. The institutions that are willing to approach the management of enrollments with creativity and a willingness to take intelligent risks are far more likely to succeed than those that attempt to copy some other institution's model.
6. Since enrollment management programs must be effective in both the short and long run, all decisions must be made with an awareness of short-range and long-range consequences.
7. Gaining the total commitment of the institution, especially the deans and faculty, is absolutely essential to the success of the program.
8. Leadership of a key university administrator is crucial to winning institutional commitment, to allocating university resources, and to sustaining effort from initial planning through implementation.

To the extent that DePaul University has been successful, it illustrated these essentials during an extraordinary period of institutional change.

Commentary by Don Hossler

The DePaul University case study offers a sharp contrast to the other three case studies. DePaul has developed the most centralized and tightly coupled enrollment management system of the four institutions examined. It also represents the only example of transformational change. Because of the nature of the changes implemented at DePaul, it has experienced the most dramatic short-term results from its enrollment management efforts.

The change model that was followed at DePaul can probably best be described as a transformational change model. Between 1979 and 1983, new student enrollment fell by almost 30 percent. The institution had attempted to become more selective during a period when the number of high school graduates was declining. In addition, the university took no steps to upgrade the admissions and financial aid offices at a time when it was attempting to compete with more institutions for more able students. Enrollment-related policies and activities were not closely linked during this period. As the result of enrollment declines, the institution perceived itself to be in a state of crisis. Threats to institutional stability were not on the horizon; they had already arrived and were having a negative impact on the health of the campus.

The identification of a crisis resulted in rapid administrative response to the problem. In the case of DePaul the academic vice president became the prime mover and chief advocate of organizational change. After being introduced to the concept of enrollment management by the director of admissions, the vice president quickly created a matrix system that included admissions, financial aid, assessment, and advising. In addition, the institutional research office was directed to focus its attention on enrollment-related issues. Other evidence of the breadth and depth of institutional response to the crisis was the involvement of the deans of the various colleges and schools and the use of forums and working papers to educate and involve all administrative areas as well as the faculty. In keeping with a transformational change model, the DePaul case study indicates that support was forthcoming from most areas of the campus. This is more readily accomplished when the conditions are ripe for transformational change.

Another key factor in bringing about the rapid change, which Patricia Ewers discusses in her case study, is that of risk taking. Instead of engaging in risk-avoidance behaviors, which is typical of educational ogranizations,

DePaul actively encouraged risk taking. Peters and Waterman (1982) assert that this is one of the hallmarks of effective organizations. It is difficult for any important changes to be implemented when institutional norms discourage risk-taking behaviors. The willingness of the academic vice president to be so directly involved in activities ranging from leading the enrollment management matrix to making presentations to the faculty helped to underscore the importance of the problem and give it visibility. These are also essential ingredients of transformational change.

Initially, DePaul established an enrollment management matrix. Moving directly to this model created direct linkages among enrollment-related issues. Typically, moving so quickly to such a centralized approach can only be accomplished in periods of institutional instability. Within 18 months of the creation of the enrollment management matrix, DePaul had decided to create an enrollment management division that would be headed by an associate vice president. This, too, happened quickly. It is also the kind of visible change that demonstrates to the campus community that campus leaders are taking direct action to ameliorate the crisis. These examples support the guidelines outlined for transformational change, which state that leaders using this strategy must take assertive and decisive actions. The movement from the matrix to the enrollment management division also demonstrates that the development of enrollment management models is frequently evolutionary. They often move from less centralized, loosely coupled structures to more centralized, tightly coupled structures. Since the chief administrator of the enrollment management division is an associate vice president, not a full vice president, the DePaul model might not be considered a pure enrollment management division as described by Kemerer, Baldridge, and Green (1982). This helps, however, to illustrate that the four models are not static, that they can be adapted to individual institutional needs.

Because DePaul is a large private institution, it illustrates how some elements of an enrollment management system can be more decentralized. Each school or college is responsible for setting its enrollment goals and helping to develop enrollment strategies. An administrator in each college is appointed to deal with enrollment-related issues. The colleges are also responsible for all follow-up activities once prospective students have been identified. In this way the admissions office, after initiating the recruitment process, serves in a more consultative role to individual departments.

DePaul has placed a geat deal of emphasis upon gathering and utilizing information to guide policy development. Patricia Ewers emphasizes the availability of relevant research, one of he eight "rules" of successful enrollment management efforts. This emphasizes the necessity of establishing a viable enrollment management plan.

Although DePaul is attempting to create a holistic enrollment management system, its greatest successes to date have been in the area of admissions management. Structurally, the university has begun to address the issue of student attrition, but it has had little impact on student persistence to date. Attention to student retention at the organizational level should enable DePaul to develop strategies to influence persistence rates; what appears to be lacking at this point are programmatic activities. As student retention programs are developed, decentralizing these programs to meet the needs of different target populations in the various schools (just as DePaul has done with the admissions area) may be the most effective approach.

Perhaps one of the most compelling aspects of the DePaul case study is the description of both the institutional and the human costs of rapidly implementing an enrollment management system. Transformational change can be very attractive to administrators because it can bring about dramatic results quickly. The risks can be high, however, and the changes do not come without making hard choices, which have costs for those required to implement the changes, as well as for those who have to make the decisions. What has happened at DePaul is a dramatic success story, but it is also a story of organizational tension and turbulence.

Chapter 6

A Case Study: The University of Wisconsin at Oshkosh

R. Thomas Snider

The enrollment history of the University of Wisconsin at Oshkosh is similar to that of many other regional public universities. Between 1869 and 1971 the institution was slowly transformed from a normal school to a comprehensive state university:

Year	Name	No. of Students
1869	Oshkosh Normal School	173
1925	Wisconsin State Teachers College	592
1949	Wisconsin State College	933
1969	Wisconsin State University at Oshkosh	11,149
1971	University of Wisconsin at Oshkosh	11,811

Between 1964 and 1969 enrollment increased 119 percent (5,375 to 11,811). No one asked how or why such growth occurred. No one attempted to control this growth or to analyze it.

For 119 years, the institution emphasized only teacher education. As a state university, its special mission had been set by its board of regents as teaching. In an attempt to limit duplication of programs, many of Wisconsin's state universities had unique special missions (vocational education, physical education, business education, etc.).

Even though the University of Wisconsin at Oshkosh had added the

R. THOMAS SNIDER is assistant to the vice chancellor for enrollment management at the University of Wisconsin at Oshkosh.

following curriculums, its public image was one of providing mainly teacher education:

1949	Liberal Arts College
1965	Business College
1966	Nursing College
1968	Master of Business Administration
1969–77	Numerous liberal arts departments

Academically, it was perceived as a good regional institution.

The city of Oshkosh (50,000) is located in the northeast section of Wisconsin, 90 miles north of Milwaukee and 90 miles northeast of Madison. A majority of the state's population lives in a corridor that makes up the eastern third of the state. The university is in this corridor.

A probable reason for the university's rapid growth was that the competition for students was low. No other higher education institutions existed in the northeast quadrant of Wisconsin until 1972. Since that time, the University of Wisconsin at Green Bay, University of Wisconsin at Fox Valley, and University of Wisconsin at Fond du Lac have been built within 50 miles of the University of Wisconsin at Oshkosh.

Between 1971 and 1977 there was a precipitous enrollment decline. The university moved from 11,811 students to 10,007—a 15 percent decline when the state of Wisconsin had a 12 percent increase in 18-year-olds. A solution to the problem was to move from an admissions policy of admitting only high school students in the upper 75 percent of their high school class to that of open admissions. It was felt that the university would attract enough students from the bottom quarter of their high school class to stop the decline. In addition, the calendar was changed from 17-17 to 14-3-14-3 weeks.

A theme was adopted labeling the university as "the university of alternatives." For various reasons, this enrollment strategy backfired. The enrollment decline continued, and a university, which has been known as a good academic institution, had changed its reputation to a school that changes images frequently. This was not a good position to be in if the public expected stability in its institution of higher education.

The characteristics of the enrollment problem included a freshman class that had slipped from 2,497 in 1971 to 1,666 in 1979. Freshman class academic quality moved from an average high school rank of 62 percent in 1971 to 56 percent in 1977. Most important, retention of freshmen to sophomore year dropped from 71 percent in 1971 to 62 percent in 1977. The decline moved to a level that was so hazardous that (with enrollment-based funding by the state) a "tenure lay off" occurred during one year.

ENROLLMENT MANAGEMENT BEGINS: NEW DIRECTOR OF ADMISSIONS

In 1977, the university administration decided that the best place to begin to change the decline was to hire a professional admissions director with a background in market analysis. Until this time, four directors had served, and each had been internal appointments.

After three months of problem analysis (market analysis) by the new director of admissions, a three-year (1977–1980) marketing plan was written. The strengths, weaknesses, and barriers to success were identified after consultation with every academic dean, departmental chairman, student service chairman, and top administrator. Campus-wide meetings were held, and all the above were invited to review the results. General agreement on the problems and their solutions emerged from those key staff members. From this process, the first step in the marketing plan was put into place— the campus was prepared to present a uniform image of its strengths to its publics.

MANAGEMENT INFORMATION SYSTEM BEGINS: A NEW ARRAY OF DATA AND DISTRIBUTION

The heart of any marketing plan must be knowing what the institution is and is not. The University of Wisconsin at Oshkosh has an institutional research office and the university system has a data information office. Much of the data needed for the profile of the institution and its student body existed, but it had not been extracted in a useful manner for managerial decision making. It had not been distributed to a wide-enough audience to develop a campus-wide awareness of problems. Therefore, managers were not sensitive to their possible roles in solutions.

A marketing research team (a systems analyst, a statistician, the director of admissions, and a computer science student) was formed to determine what data existed and in what form. Needs were defined and new reports were formatted. The audience was defined as the director of admissions and key institutional decision makers (chancellor, vice chancellor, deans, directors, and department chairpersons). Exception reporting was adopted for the director of admissions, and trend reporting was adopted for the campus.

Biweekly reports from the director of admissions to those key staff members were instituted. Graphs were used for ease of communication. A three-year plan of reporting was adopted:

—Year 1: Educate the admissions staff as to the present student body profile and applicants' profile.

—Year 2: Emphasize which students succeed on campus and highlight those applicant statistics.

—Year 3: Disaggregate enrollments to emphasize enrollment trends for minority groups and individual academic programs.

During this three-year period, an on-line applicant and prospect system was developed. The major feature of this program was the electronic tracking of all university recruiting efforts for every prospect and applicant. Our file has approximately 25,000 prospective student names and 3,300 applicant names. Three hundred separate activities can be tracked and evaluated as to their success in converting prospects to applicants and applicants to enrollees (presently we have a 61 percent yield from applicant to enrolled versus a 43 percent yield in 1978).

Zero-based budgeting occurs each year, and the reporting system described above helps to determine which activities will be continued, eliminated, or modified.

KNOWING THE EXTERNAL MARKET

The marketing research team next analyzed the external environment. Our university system has an extensive data collection process from each of its 14 campuses. The reports, which are then given to each campus, are:

1. Monthly system application and admission reports by campus
2. Periodic monthly multiple application reports (percentage of applications a campus has that are single applications to the system, etc.)
3. Wisconsin population reports
4. A report that identifies two-year college students' intentions as to which University of Wisconsin campus they wish to transfer to
5. Department of Public Instruction high school population reports

A missing component was, What was the reputation of the institution? It had not been assessed. Therefore, the marketing team developed a three-year study of how various publics perceived the university. In particular, the following studies were conducted:

1. Geographic (regional counties and high schools)
2. Applicants who enrolled
3. Applicants who did not enroll
4. Parents (of those who did and did not enroll)
5. High school counselors

After analysis, our hypothesis was confirmed that the academic reputation of the university was damaged by the previously mentioned "open admission" approach. Instead of increasing the number of freshmen, a decline in class size continued. All that had occurred was that the university's profile traded freshmen in the top 10 percent of their high school class for the bottom 10 percent. It traded a good academic reputation for one that the public perceived as taking anyone into its fold. The marketing studies confirmed this perception of the university by its primary and secondary markets. The weaker academic credentials of the students created new problems:

1. Lower faculty morale. The majority of this faculty had been hired from 1964 to 1971 (during the population increase from 5,375 to 11,811 students). Their academic credentials were unusually strong. One explanation for this was that they were hired with the possibility of the university adding doctoral programs in their fields. This attracted young professors who wanted to be a part of building such a program from scratch. Then, the board of regents determined that only two campuses in the system (Madison and Milwaukee) would offer doctorates. In addition to this disappointment, the undergraduate student body they were teaching had weaker high school credentials.
2. Attrition from freshman to sophomore year was 34 percent (much greater than the 29 percent national average).
3. The academic atmosphere had been eroded. A party school image was emerging. St. Patrick's Day parties in Oshkosh became so widely known that Johnny Carson suggested that "If you can't be in Ireland today, go to Oshkosh."

UNIVERSITY-WIDE GOAL SETTING

In 1978, a new chancellor was named, and his first goal was to bring everyone together in a campus-wide conference to set new goals. He used the Delphi technique[1] to achieve this.

Some individuals approached that conference with the idea that its report would be made only to be filed away. The chancellor assured everyone that this was not the case. He related that the goals set in the conference would determine budgets and structure evaluations of individuals. Once it was realized by the assembled body that this was a no-nonsense, real exercise, the group went to work.

It is important to realize that a goal is something that is achievable, but not easily. A goal must be measurable so you can determine whether you

---

1. For a complete discussion of the Delphi technique see *Futurism in Education: Methodologies* (1974) by S. F. Henckley and J. R. Yates.

have reached it or not. A goal has someone responsible for it so that responsibility can be assessed.

In order to achieve goals that were universally accepted, the conference participants represented faculty members, administrators, academic staff, and students. In other words, the whole university felt involved. This was an intense exercise that took place during a break at the university so that the assembled body could meet for many hours during a number of consecutive days. They looked at the strengths of the university and at its weaknesses. They looked at the goals they would like to achieve and the barriers that could prevent them from achieving those goals. Many goals were set. Many goals were combined. The goals were then sifted and made to fit the criteria mentioned earlier. Were the goals of the university such that they would make the institution grow? Would they be measurable? Would there be an individual or division responsible for each goal? The goals then were ranked in order of importance.

At the end of this exercise, the report from the conference was sent to every individual in the university so they could comment on it and rank the goals in order of importance. They could also add goals. This will be familiar to some as the Delphi technique.

After this exercise, the original group was brought together again to try to democratically interpret the voting of the rest of the institution. Following this meeting, a revised set of goals were sent back to all governance groups in the university, and finally, our goals were set.

The goals at our institution are consensual goals. Every manager in the university understands what they are. Every manager is asked to build his or her budget each year with these goals in mind. If in a scarce resource environment there is a choice between projects, the project with the higher priority goal will be funded.

There were 14 university goals and, in order of importance, they covered enrollment, minimum competencies, teaching excellence, retention, professional activity, quality assurance, foundation in the arts and sciences, university environment, ethics and values, public service, shared governance, community, and affirmative action.

Institutional research was charged to develop a quantitative tracking system such that managers would receive feedback regarding their efforts in each area. In addition, the chancellor would then have data to plot success in each area so that his budget decisions could be based on this information.

Our development of each goal is the basis of our success in enrollment management. To illustrate, the retention and enrollment goals will be used.

Enrollment management means that a university needs the ability to have greater control over its environment. It means that there is a need to effectively manage enrollment, not have the enrollment manage the university. It means that the board goal of management is to redefine enrollment goals and to achieve the upper hand in effectively determining the destiny of the university. Enrollment management is really an elusive and confusing proposition. It is more than a simple renaming and reordering of existing structures and functions.

RETENTION GOAL

The retention goal was stated thus: "The university will strengthen its retention of students by increasing the retention rate of full-time freshmen by one point five percent (1.5%) per year for each of the next six years."

To attack this problem, a faculty committee was charged with the responsibility of retention. Kemerer, Baldridge, and Green (1982) suggest that faculty have other duties and may treat such an approach as just another committee assignment, resulting in very little being accomplished. However, if administrators solely own the retention problem and the faculty does not, retention really will not change. Administrators can put in all sorts of wonderful structures, but in the end it is the faculty's impact on students that affects retention.

In fact, the faculty has proposed a number of retention ideas that they own, but now there is an administrator, the assistant to the vice chancellor, to follow through in structuring these ideas into a working program. A few of these areas are:

1. Reinstating midterm grades for all freshman and sophomore courses. Any student with one or more D's at midterm time is called in by the academic adviser for consultation.
2. Identification of the 200 freshmen most likely to drop out of the university. Institutional research identified these students, and we have placed them in a program called the "assistance program." These students are light-loaded; they are required to take all the basic skills courses they need, and they are required to sign a contract stating that they will come in once a month and see their adviser to bring them up to date as to whether they are succeeding in school.
3. Early identification of all "undecided on a major" students among the entering freshmen, and development of an intrusive counseling program for them. Twenty percent of our freshman class were undecided about their majors. This is a group that is likely to drop out of school. Therefore, on the day of their registration for classes, we "pull them out of the group" for special advising. They go through an exercise in which they place themselves into one of four groups: (1) decided,

but undeclared; (2) so many interests that I can't decide; (3) wanting a degree but few strong interests; and (4) not certain. Three for-credit courses were created (career planning, higher education and you, and comprehensive study skills) to meet the above students' needs. They are advised to enroll in one or more of the above courses. Also, our career advising program, career software program, and placement services are explained.

During the fall semester, undecided students are followed up by the counseling staff for further counseling. In addition, a career news-letter was created for them.

4. A cueing system (using the ACT or SAT profile) was developed for academic advising. High school students fill out a profile about them-selves when they take the ACT or SAT. Too few schools use these profiles. There are many "cues" to the likely attrition of certain students. Advisers seldom use the profiles because of their workloads and the amount of data that they have on each student (too much). Therefore, we extracted only student data that reflected potential problems. The computer was programmed to print only aberrant data: i.e., expects an A average in college but only had a B average in high school; wants to be an engineer but will major in music; predicted to have less than a C in a certain course; says he needs help in mathe-matics; wants to "join the band." The adviser uses this information to help the student to be involved in the "right" activities at the begin-ning of college as well as to help the student to be as realistic about his goals as possible.

Our results have been successful:

Freshmen to Sophomore Retention Rates

1977–78	62%
1978–79	63
1979–80	64
1980–81	65
1981–82	66
1982–83	68
1983–84	71
1984–85	72

ENROLLMENT GOAL

The enrollment goal was: "The university will enhance its service to the region by increasing the admission of freshmen graduating in the upper 40 percent of their high school class, increasing the number from its service region, etc. . . ." No one person could achieve these goals. Without a structural change to an enrollment management model, how could we achieve this goal? We decided to approach it in the following ways:

1. *Marketing plan.* The director of admissions developed a plan approved by the chancellor, deans, and faculty. The goal was to help students through the college decision process in a personalized way. This meant that 300 faculty became involved in the process as well as 600 alumni and 300 students. In addition, the following were developed:
   a. On-line prospect system
   b. On-line applicant system
   c. Electronic tracking system of all admission activities
   d. Continuous registration system that allows high school seniors to register for their freshman year courses in small groups during their senior year in high school.

2. *Faculty admissions committee to enact admissions policy changes.* Many times directors of admissions feel that they cannot effect academic change on their campus. This is not true. They must work, formally and informally, with all governance groups and deans.

   We have an admissions committee on this campus that is composed of faculty and students. We have tackled our goal of improving the quality of the entering class slowly and introduced approximately one change each year since 1978 that has dramatically affected our campus. In effect, this group is a lobbying group for academic change to the faculty governance groups. Changes started in this committee are:

1978   Raised standards for good academic standing for continuing students
1979   Created Honors Scholarship Program
1980   Raised admissions requirements so that all matriculants had to have graduated in the upper 75 per cent of their class (the institution had previously been open admissions)
1980   Created an honors college for students in the upper 10 percent of their high school class.
1981   Required ACT/SAT
1982   Instituted an early warning system
1985   Changed admission requirements to increase the years of high school courses required for entrance.

The university is attracting better applicants. They are staying with us, getting involved in our programs, and pressing us to keep doing better what we already do well—teach, carry out research, and provide service to our region.

When we set stricter standards for good academic standing, and increased advising and counseling opportunities, attrition fell.

When we instituted our Honors Scholarships, we attracted numbers of highly qualified student recipients (we began with 20 such scholarships; in 1985–86 that number hit 37). Even more significant, better than 75 percent of all the students competing for those scholarships (some 300 each year) have decided to enroll at the university, even though they did not win a scholarship.

When we began our University Scholars Program, some 218 new freshmen met the eligibility requirement (graduation in the upper 10 percent of their high school class). This academic year, the university has more than 420 enrolled in this program.

When we raised our high school rank requirement, our student applicant pool expanded. Not only did quality rise, but so did numbers. Our average high school rank is now at the 62nd percentile versus the 56th percentile in 1977.

Though the early warning system was instituted as a means of offering our students better information and academic advising, it has had a significant effect in terms of reducing attrition from the university. It has focused student attention on academic performance and the need for strong study skills.

When the university required that entering students for the 1986–87 academic year must have completed a set of solid high school courses, there was some concern that the number of new students would plunge. Precisely the opposite has happened. Though almost three times as many aspiring freshmen as at this time last year have been denied admission, our applications are up some 26 percent. The number of applicants graduating in the upper 25 percent of their high school class has increased by 26 percent.

University of Wisconsin at Oshkosh became a sponsor of National Merit Awards this year. This fall, 1986, there will be five National Merit award winners on campus.

Has our reputation changed? Yes. A research paper done by the market research team has determined that our publics rate us a "B+" in academic strength in relation to our competition.

Have all our goals been achieved? Partially. However, that is not the point. The point is that our university as a whole has made a positive statement about controlling its own environment. Yes, we did set some goals that were, in retrospect, unrealistic. Yes, a few of those goals were very difficult to measure, but we are aware of them and constantly revising our thoughts about them. Presently, we are readying ourselves for a new university-wide goal-setting exercise in the fall. In enrollment management, that is half the battle—knowing who you are and where you want to be.

MATRIX STAFFING

Can an enrollment model work without forming an enrollment division? Yes. We have used the existing reporting structure but employ a matrix *staffing* approach. For the last four years, the admissions office worked hand-in-hand with the financial aid office and our advising area in cross-training staff so that they are able to work in all three offices. For example, an admissions counselor responsible for recruiting minorities trains in the financial aid office. One goal of our institution is to increase minority students, and we know that financial aid is one of the most important areas to understand for an individual with the responsibility for minority recruitment. If that individual works with the financial aid office and totally understands packaging and the application flow from the minority student to the university, then all the better.

Also, we have a multicultural center whose goal is to bring different cultures together. The Indian and Hispanic advisers work in the admissions office for part of their contract.

In addition, we have three staff members who are assigned to the advisement office during times when we are registering our entering students. They are highly aware of the problems incoming freshmen have and are very strong communicators to both the advising and admissions staffs regarding problems each might create for the other. Three athletic assistant coaches work in the admissions office during their "off season." Below is a summary of matrix staffing:

Staff member 1 = 10% financial aid, 60% general admissions, 30% minority admissions
Staff member 2 = 25% advising, 75% admissions
Staff member 3 = 20% advising, 80% admissions
Staff members 4, 5 = 90% multicultural advising, 10% admissions
Staff members 6, 7 = 50% athletics, 50% admissions

All matrix staff have dual reporting and attend as many staff meetings of each office as they can. The interchange of ideas and problems has been invaluable. We are effecting a better environment for student success at the university by this linkage.

We have a central advising area for all freshmen and sophomores prior to choosing their academic majors. It is unique in the sense that we have a completely on-line computer registration system that has existed for the last eight years. Our registrar is also the director of advising, and we have a large area where 10 full-time advisers' offices and the terminals used for registration are located. After students see their adviser, they step out of the office, walk to a terminal, and register.

We start to register our student body for the following fall in February. Therefore, we are able to register approximately 100 upper-class students per day over a long period of time so that each individual student receives personal attention. We have 70 percent of our fall freshman class registered by June 1. This unique advising system brings in 30 to 40 high school seniors per day to choose their courses for the following fall.

Public universities are sometimes viewed as impersonal places. By working with a few students each day over a long period of time, we have changed that reputation for our institution. This has positively affected our recruitment.

It also has allowed us to take control of our environment. By having just a few students register each day, the deans can watch courses and see how they are being filled. As a result, large numbers of courses do not close all at once and disappoint students. By registering substantial numbers of the student body prior to June 1, we stop registering students for the month of June and reassess the whole registration situation. Completely new courses for the fall can be arranged, if neccessary. Students who register this way have a very high show-up rate in the fall. They feel a commitment to returning the following year. They feel a commitment to go directly from high school to our institution. They have invested a lot of themselves in that advising time and have a class schedule. Therefore, the movement from one year to the next is an orderly one.

A dramatic turnabout in enrollment from 10,007 (1977) to 11,800 (1985) has occurred.

MANAGEMENT INFORMATION SYSTEM

The number of automated systems developed by each enrollment management team (in admissions, financial aid, orientation, registration, advising, housing, career counseling, and bookstore) needed to be integrated. We needed a management system that provided managers with information to support their routine decision system. In addition, we needed interactive systems that provided easy access to decision models and data supporting semistructured decision making and planning. These systems needed to be accessed and used via on-line terminals.

We knew that it was not possible to build, at a reasonable cost, an effective management information system for an organization that did not have a set of commonly accepted, well-defined goals. However, our goals were well defined, staffs were matrixed, faculty and academic staffs were working together, our computer hardware and software were up to date, and we had a good analyst, yet we could not achieve a management information system (MIS) program. Put simply, our current managers were not familiar with decision-making tools that were available to them. They are very busy individuals with little time and financial resources available for reeducating themselves to managing information electronically. They were often at a stage in their professional careers when the prospect of learning a new trick (with a computer) was not attractive. However, we could not afford not to use the information and decision support at our disposal.

We attacked the personnel problem by:

1. Forming a management information system institute (Koehn Institute) on our campus, which reviews all new microcomputer hardware and software on the market. It serves the business community as well as our campus community.
2. Changing some of our reporting system from paper to "floppy disk," which forced managers to learn "new tricks."
3. Offering "free" services to offices that utilized new software programs.
4. Presenting "free" short courses during office time to learn new software.
5. Using key offices as models and using those managers as peer teachers.

We, like our counterparts in the business sector, must decide to replace or retrofit. We should be able to do the latter. After all, our business is education.

An example of this approach is the system the admissions office, registrar, advisers, and bookstore developed. This program, *Class Level Index Program,* helps our deans to make decisions during our continuous registration process (registration for a single semester over a three- to six-month period prior to that semester). We can now predict each week that, if we continue to have students enrolled for certain courses at the same rate, the percent full level the following fall will be above or below 100 percent. Advisers meet each Friday to look at the course full prediction. They can move students into areas where the percent full level is significantly below the predicted 100 percent full level. The deans can add courses slowly during this process, and, therefore, employ staff in an efficient manner.

An automatic book order system is hooked into the above program. As the deans add seats or sections, book orders are placed so all students will have books at the opening of school.

Another example is our enrollment prediction model. We have written a program that predicts enrollment to the year 2000. From this prediction, we can predict credit production and then instructional full-time equivalents (iFTE) necessary to teach them. Another model is drawn off this system—a capacity model. It is important for our university to maintain its quality teaching. Therefore, we do not allow the "free market" enrollment prediction model to solely determine decisions for our deans and administration. The capacity model takes into account a cap of iFTE/student credit hours and a quality level of student body.

The future of our organization and management information system rests in our ability to learn to adapt the technologies to our purpose.

ENROLLMENT MANAGEMENT STRUCTURE

Our present structure has been dictated by our evolution in enrollment management. We, very deliberately, have involved our whole campus in the process. We have an Admissions Committee, Academic Review Committee, all student service offices, Deans' Council, Faculty Senate, Faculty Retention Committee, and academic departments all involved. By appointing an assistant to the vice chancellor for enrollment management, the university acknowledged a coordinator of this effort. As an assistant to the chief academic officer of the university, the university was stating that this staff person headed a university-wide effort in which the faculty were a key to success.

An example of the new, coordinated enrollment management change was the discovery by the Admissions Committee of how a liberal course drop policy was creating 2,700 vacant classroom seats at the end of a semester. With enrollment at near maximum, this policy was not only preventing students who were denied access to those seats at the beginning of the semester from taking courses they wanted, but creating a poor image in the community (students could not get the courses they needed). This could effect a drop in the number of new students if not remedied. The liberal arts dean was given a report to this effect, and he proposed to the appropriate governance group to change the policy to a shorter withdrawal time. He estimates this change will save 10 instructional FTE, which will allow him to "put up" new courses and decrease class section sizes in popular majors. This was a team approach to solving a potentially large problem.

Now that enrollment is at an all-time high, with a student academic profile as strong as it has ever been, and retention figures above the national average, will we make the same mistake we made earlier—relax? No, we know why we are succeeding. We will continue to anticipate the future needs of our public and meet them.

Commentary by Don Hossler

The University of Wisconsin at Oshkosh case study provides an opportunity to analyze an enrollment management system that has been evolving for several years. Like the DePauw University case study that follows, Oshkosh is an example of the accrual model of change. The activities that have become part of the responsibilities of the assistant to the vice chancellor for enrollment management have accrued to Tom Snider over a period of 10 years. The university did not start out with the intention of creating an enrollment management division; nevertheless, this is now the term they use to describe their comprehensive program.

The enrollment management efforts at Oshkosh have been successful. Since 1977, through the use of a systematic approach to marketing, recruitment, and retention, the university has been able to raise the quality of its students, increase the number of students by 15 percent, and reduce its attrition rate by 10 percent. Goals related to student enrollments and strategies to achieve those goals are built into the planning process each year. This assures that institutional decision makers will consider the effects of their decisions on student enrollments.

The impetus for many of the steps taken by the university to develop their current enrollment management system was an enrollment decline. Although the decline did not threaten the existence of the institution, it was of sufficient magnitude that tenured faculty members had to be released. Declining enrollments had attracted the attention of the entire campus. The arrival of a new chancellor and the campus-wide goal-setting process became the catalyst in creating a supportive environment for change.

The Oshkosh case study demonstrates how the development of an enrollment management system can be seen as an iterative process. Since declining enrollments was a major problem, this is the area that first received attention. However, student attrition rates were also high and retention goals and programming quickly followed efforts in the admissions area. Later in the evolution of the program at Wisconsin, academic programs were put into place to attract better students and to change the academic image of the campus. More recently management information systems have been developed that have further enhanced the enrollment management system at the university. Each of these steps was part of the evolving enrollment-related activities designed to increase student enroll-ments, as well as to attract more students with the characteristics desired by the institution.

The importance of the involvement of faculty is evident in this case study. Faculty took the lead in developing student retention programs. These programs range from an "early warning" system to identify potential dropouts to an intrusive advising system for students with undeclared majors. Educating faculty about the factors that influence enrollments and involving them in solving enrollment-related problems is a prominent fea-ture of an effective enrollment management system.

This case study reinforces the importance of information in the devel-opment of an enrollment management system. The collection and dissem-ination of market and retention research plays a prominent role in the system that has developed at Oshkosh. Snider suggests that student en-rollment research was the basis for efforts to alter the image of the campus, changes in the admissions standards, the introduction of a new advising program, and the targeting of a subpopulation of students for academic assistance.

Of the four case studies presented, Oshkosh has developed the most comprehensive management information system. They have developed on-line tracking systems for admissions and financial aid and a continuous registration system that provides information to faculty for advising as well as making the entire course selection process much easier for students. Oshkosh has stressed the importance of information in decision making at all levels of administration. Its decentralized information network is im-pressive as are its attempts to make the software and user applications accessible to everyone. The linkages between enrollments and academic planning are apparent; the registration system permits sounder staffing decisions for class offerings. Even textbook ordering is tied into this en-rollment-driven management information system. The on-line information system at the university is used to improve the quality of student life and enhance student satisfaction in areas such as advising, course selection, and even the availability of textbooks. This computer system and its applications are a hallmark of the Oshkosh model.

Although Tom Snider's new title would suggest that the university has adopted the centralized enrollment management division model, there are no pure models. The Oshkosh model is a combination of the enrollment management division and a matrix model. The matrix staffing pattern in admissions, which links admissions to financial aid, minority and multicultural affairs, and athletics, demonstrates the unique qualities that each campus-based system may develop.

The enrollment management system at the University of Wisconsin at Oshkosh is not a static, closed plan. As evidenced by some of the most recent changes, it is still evolving. The system is dynamic, constantly refining questions and programs. Through the use of the kind of process analysis described by Gratz and Salem (see Chapter 2), administrators at Oshkosh should ensure that they will be able to continue to influence their enrollments.

Chapter 7

A Case Study: DePauw University

David Murray

DePauw University was founded in 1837, and like nearly all of the colleges of that era it was founded by a religious denomination, in this case the Methodists. DePauw retains its affiliation with the Methodist Church, although today on the surface the affiliation sometimes appears to be a nominal one.

In part, this impression is attributable to the original charter, which stated that the university was "forever to be conducted on the most liberal principles, accessible to all religious denominations, and designed for the benefit of our citizens in general." The Methodists had been frustrated in their attempts to enroll their sons (women were admitted to DePauw earlier than most places, but not until 1867) in the colleges of other religious denominations, so the university's ecumenical foundation was laid intentionally. Today, of about 2,300 students enrolled each year, 22 percent are Catholic, 20 percent are Methodist, and almost every Judeo-Christian denomination is represented.

One of the most significant legacies of DePauw's ecumenical Methodism is the university's commitment to values and ethics. It surfaces in the university's graduation requirements, as well as in the character and activities of its student body.

Like many of the old-line schools, DePauw went through periods of prosperity and economic hardship. In the early years the church was the university's primary financial benefactor, but as time went on, DePauw began to develop a very loyal following of alumni and friends.

DAVID MURRAY became director of admissions at DePauw University in 1978. In 1983 he was named assistant vice president for enrollment and administrative planning.

Originally founded as Indiana Asbury, the name was changed to DePauw University in 1884. During the economic depression of the 1870s, Indiana Asbury was rescued from economic hardship by Washington C. DePauw whose gifts, together with those of his family, totaled about $600,000. The trustees authorized the change in the name from Indiana Asbury to De-Pauw University, but the original name survives in the Asbury College of Liberal Arts, where about 90 percent of DePauw's students are enrolled.

Interestingly, W. C. DePauw and other members of his family took a special interest in the creation, in 1884, of one of DePauw's two professional schools, the School of Music, which today enrolls about 125 students. The other professional school in existence today is the School of Nursing with approximately 100 students. It was founded in 1955 and the nursing curriculum, like the music curriculum, has a strong foundation in the liberal arts.

The gifts made by Washington C. DePauw and his family were typical of the kind of loyalty and support the institution was destined to receive from its alumni and friends for generations to come, but an especially important gift to the university occurred in 1919. Edward Rector, a patent attorney in Chicago, and his wife established the Edward Rector Scholarship Foundation.

Nearly $2.5 million was given to establish this foundation and instantly DePauw was able to offer full-tuition scholarships to every valedictorian and salutatorian in the state of Indiana. In the early years sufficient funds existed to make the same kind of offer to some students from outside Indiana. For decades the scholarships were made available only to men because the university had particular difficulty in attracting men at the time of the original gift; today Rector Scholarships are given to both men and women. The Rector Scholarship program was a major factor in DePauw's weathering of the Depression years and it was a key ingredient for several decades in DePauw's financial and enrollment stability, as well as its prestige.

Like all colleges and universities, DePauw enjoyed the enrollment advantages of the 1960s, but with the beginning of the demographic decline of the mid-1970s, it became increasingly clear the university had reached a new turning point. Although DePauw's traditional liberal arts program continued to be strong, people began to feel there was more that could be done to complement the traditional program with new academic opportunities. Faculty began to think about reinstituting distribution requirements and adding new graduation requirements. People also wondered if there was not more DePauw could be doing to help its students prepare and compete for graduate school and employment opportunities.

DePauw's enrollment has remained steady for the last few decades.

Shortly after the School of Nursing was added in 1955, the enrollment rose to about 2,200 students. Over the roughly 30 years that have followed, the number of full-time equivalent (FTE) students has fluctuated between about 2,200 and 2,400. From a high of 2,422 FTE in 1967–68, enrollment dropped as low as 2,174 FTE in 1973–74.

Applications for admission also gradually decreased over the same period. When the national decline in the tested ability of high school seniors was added to DePauw's less selective posture, the average credentials of entering classes declined noticeably over time.

Concurrently, DePauw's costs began to escalate. From a base in 1957–58 of $600, DePauw's tuition increased only $100 each year until 1967–68, when it reached $1,600. Then it took only six years to increase another $1,050 by 1973–74. Thirteen years later, tuition has been set at $8,200 for 1986–87. Room and board adds another $3,215. Books, travel, and personal expenses must be added on top of that.

In the mid-1970s, the Rector Scholarship program was still the primary scholarship endowment and working off the original principal of about $2.5 million. Given the dramatic increase in DePauw's costs since 1919, the monies involved no longer went nearly as far as they once did. In addition, DePauw's physical plant was ready for, and in need of, the next generation of facilities.

About this same time, DePauw's president retired and the college prepared for its next generation of leadership. The trustees made their selection and in February 1977 DePauw's seventeenth president took over. It was obvious his leadership would be crucial where DePauw's enrollment stability and the overall quality of the university were concerned.

NEW LEADERSHIP

In looking back now almost a decade later, it seems remarkable what has been accomplished in a relatively short time. No formal enrollment management plan has ever been instituted—the term, enrollment management, is rarely even used in conversation—but clearly DePauw developed its own informal plan.

Faculty reinstituted distribution requirements, including courses that must examine the ethical considerations involved in studying various disciplines, to ensure a liberal arts education. The 4-1-4 calendar with a one-course block of study in January was instituted, and internships were eventually allowed as an accepted form of educational experience during this one-month semester.

In ways that attracted national attention, steps were taken to ensure that all students would be competent in writing, quantitative reasoning, and self-expression. New graduation requirements demand competency in these areas and study centers support the efforts of students.

The faculty also established the Center for Management and Entrepreneurship with an honors program called the Management Fellows program as a part of it. Semester-long, paid internships for Management Fellows at top firms, many of them Fortune 500 companies, complement the traditional liberal arts classes offered to Management Fellows or any other student at the university. This center is now endowed and each year about 90 percent of the students admitted as Management Fellows enroll, selecting DePauw over some of the most prestigious schools in the country.

Similarly, faculty developed the Honor Scholar program. Loosely described as a "great books" seminar program, students participate in seminars the first two years, then apprentice themselves to a faculty mentor of the student's choice for the junior and senior years. The last two years are spent in study, research, and writing, leading to an honors thesis that frequently has been publishable. This program often appeals to the student who has a real love of ideas and is interested in the most liberal of educations.

In January 1985, the board of trustees announced the new, endowed Center for Contemporary Media, which will be established to build on historic liberal arts strengths and complement traditional classroom activities. Sigma Delta Chi, the largest United States journalism honorary society, was founded at DePauw in 1909, and currently DePauw is the site of the Hall of Fame for journalism in the state of Indiana. The university also hosts a national undergraduate honors conference in the communications field each spring. Rich traditions like these make the development of the Center for Contemporary Media a natural extension. The fact that it will be a state-of-the-art facility (television studio, radio studio, computer graphics, darkroom and film-making capabilities, etc.), with co-curricular programs that will complement what already is happening in the classroom, is an exciting prospect. While the faculty and DePauw's academic administration have been working on these and other important curricular and cocurricular developments, DePauw also has been working on its physical plant, fund-raising, and admissions needs.

In 1977 the first priority for DePauw's new president and DePauw's development staff was to take care of the next generation of physical plant. A new $7.5 million Science and Mathematics Center had been constructed just prior to the new president's arrival. Since then the university has renovated its oldest remaining building, East College. A campus focal point and national historic landmark dating back to 1869, East College is now fully restored, inside and out, thanks to about $3 million in gifts from supportive alumni and friends.

On top of that the new $8.2 million Performing Arts Center and the $7.2 million Lilly Athletic Center have been added. This left only the renovation of DePauw's library (beginning in the summer of 1986) and one classroom building to assure DePauw's physical plant for the next several decades; thus DePauw's fund-raisers turned their attention to the next major challenge, significantly increasing DePauw's endowment.

In April 1983, DePauw's board of trustees announced a $90 million sesquicentennial campaign to be completed by 1987. At the time, it was the largest fund-raising effort ever undertaken by an undergraduate, liberal arts college. In January 1985, the board of trustees decided to raise the goal to $100 million because there were additional donors still to be contacted and gifts had already approached the $90 million mark. In October 1985, the trustees announced they had already completed the sesquicentennial campaign, nearly two years ahead of DePauw's sesquicentennial celebration.

The seeds of this exceptional financial support are twofold. First, 80 to 85 percent of an entering class at DePauw lists the university as its first choice; thus the unusual loyalty of DePauw's graduates begins at an early juncture. The succeeding four years usually further those feelings and this is a key ingredient in DePauw's ability to raise money for facilities, endowment, and its academic program.

The second reason for this unusual support goes back, interestingly enough, to the Rector Scholarship Foundation. The unusual success of DePauw's graduates, success disproportionate to their numbers, is attributable in part to the outstanding high school students the Rector program helped to attract. Recent third-party studies, each using different criteria to measure success, have ranked DePauw and its graduates' achievements among the top schools of its kind. Now, many of these former Rector Scholars are in a position to make a DePauw education possible for future generations of DePauw students through their gifts, and clearly many of them are doing just that.

New academic vision and the results of the dramatic infusion of new funds into the university have been crucial to DePauw's management of its enrollment. In fact, in some ways it is the bottom line because these days most prospective students and their parents take a very close look at any college or university before making a final decision.

Concurrent with these developments, DePauw's admissions office changed its approach to recruiting students rather significantly and that, after all, is where the whole enrollment management process begins.

ADMISSIONS

Having almost quadrupled inquiries from high school seniors, applications for admission have nearly doubled in the last seven years. DePauw received 2,287 applications for admission for fall 1985, compared with only 1,286 for fall 1978. Selectivity has soared and average combined SAT scores for entering freshmen have risen over 70 points. This dramatic improvement in the admissions situation has become self-reinforcing and is the result of both admissions-related efforts and the perception by more and more students (and their families) that DePauw's academic program and the entire experience at the university are increasingly attractive.

In analyzing DePauw's admissions program it is difficult to identify which specific activities have paid the greatest dividends, but several will be mentioned here. One of the first and most significant activities the admissions office undertook was the development of a comprehensive data system to meet the office's needs. Previously, inquiries from students and their families were handled largely through a manual process. The new data system dramatically improved the ability of the admissions office to handle contacts from students and their families in an efficient manner, supporting a host of new efforts.

Through the use of the College Board's Student Search Service and the increased use of its most loyal resources—students, faculty, and alumni— DePauw was able to increase dramatically the number of students on its mailing list. In 1978 DePauw had just over 5,000 students on its mailing list. For fall 1985, DePauw handled almost 21,000 inquiries from high school seniors. The data system has not only been crucial in communicating with the increased number of prospective students, but it also has been crucial in evaluating movements (potential cause and effect relationships) in the inquiry pool and the success or failure of various admissions activities in turning inquiries into applicants or accepted students into matriculants.

Once the new data system was in place, it enabled the admissions staff to target its travel better. During 1978–79 the staff did only about one-third of the travel it had done in previous years, but the travel was targeted more effectively. Printouts were used to analyze how many students had inquired from a given high school. Further breakdowns allowed the staff member responsible for a specific high school or geographic area to analyze the strength of the students' interest in DePauw.

For example, two high schools with the same number of students who had inquired about the university might have very different admissions potentials. One school might have a high percentage of students who had responded to direct mail activities, while the other might have a high percentage of students who had initiated contact with DePauw by letter or by sending standardized test scores to the university. The latter school would represent greater potential because more students had sought out DePauw for themselves. Admissions officers now were able to make decisions based on objective data, as well as subjective impressions.

The data system also became the basis for several research activities. Questionnaires were developed for students who had applied, both those who decided to matriculate and those who decided to go elsewhere. The staff wanted to know why students were choosing to enroll at the university and why they decided not to come. Subsequently, research activities were expanded to find out why students on the mailing list did not follow through and apply for admission. DePauw's research activities have expanded to the point that, in January 1985, a full-time director of enrollment research position was created, in addition to another office on campus already concerned with institutional research in general.

Why do all this research? Certainly in the case of matriculants the admissions staff wants to know what is attracting them to the university. Equally important, they want to know why students are not coming to DePauw. Where students have misconceptions about the university or where students do not understand DePauw's particular strengths in meeting their needs, the university must be more articulate.

A good example of the value of the research is the primary reason each year why students do not apply or why they do apply but do not attend if admitted. Year in and year out the top concern is the cost of a DePauw education. The result of this research finding is that publications have been revamped and DePauw has begun to segment its markets. In this case, for example, those who are concerned about cost are segmented from those who are not. New publications have been developed to address the specific needs or misperceptions of students and their families. Not surprisingly, more than one publication now deals with concerns about the cost of a DePauw education, as well as the value received for the investment made by any student or family, whether they pay the full comprehensive fee or only part of it as the result of financial aid.

A key point in all of this is that to approach enrollment management considerations thoughtfully, the college has to know why students make the choices they make. Once that information is known, and for those students for whom DePauw is appropriate, the school must be as articulate as possible about its strengths as they relate to the particular interests and needs of the students involved.

As a result of the student choice data collected, DePauw graduates were organized into an alumni admissions program, which now has over 500 alumni admissions representatives. Current students also were organized through the DePauw Ambassadors Club, an organization of about 250 students who host prospective students overnight, assist with campus visitation days, give tours of the campus, telephone prospective students, etc.

Another very important admissions activity has served to broaden the geographic base from which DePauw draws students and has involved the combined efforts of DePauw's alumni and its current students. In fall 1979, the first Thanksgiving receptions were formulated and held. On the basis of research done to identify developmental markets, areas with significant admissions potential for DePauw, admissions officers encouraged current students home on Thanksgiving break and local alumni to host an afternoon or evening reception for prospective students and their parents. A member of the admissions staff was present to show slides of the campus and answer some of the more technical questions, but the primary purpose was to get prospective students and their parents together with DePauw's enthusiastic students and alumni. These programs have proved contagious to the point that DePauw clubs around the country now sponsor 30 to 40 Thanksgiving receptions each year. When you combine these receptions with the efforts of the alumni admissions representatives, the activities of the DePauw Ambassadors Club, and the efforts of the admissions staff in various developmental markets, it is not surprising DePauw has experienced a significant increase in applications. Nearly all of the increase in applications has come from outside Indiana and much of it has come from outside the Midwest.

When one analyzes DePauw's success in better managing its enrollment, one crucial area cannot be overlooked, the efforts made to improve the match between DePauw and the students who enroll. Several years ago DePauw made a staffing commitment to support the logistics involved in its student–parent day and individual overnight programs. The first program typically occurs on a Saturday several times during the year and a variety of campus resources are brought together to help prospective students and their parents quickly and comprehensively investigate DePauw. During the program they have an opportunity to meet with people from the president of the university on down, including DePauw students, faculty, and staff.

With the individual overnight programs, students stay overnight with a current DePauw student, usually one of the DePauw ambassadors. With a few hundred students volunteering each year to host overnight guests, any number of prospective students are routinely accommodated and a personalized itinerary is set up for each student's stay. Students who participate in one of these programs tend to apply for admission in very high percentages and, once they are admitted, they enroll in very high percentages as well.

When students and their parents visit DePauw, the college sells itself, but the university goes to these great lengths to help the students as much as itself. It wants them to find out what DePauw is, as well as what it is not. If the students discover that DePauw is not the right place for them, the college wants that to happen before they enroll.

These campus visit programs have been instrumental in enhancing and reinforcing other recruiting activities, and thus increasing DePauw's applicant pool, but undoubtedly these programs also have been a factor in students making intelligent decisions about DePauw. They are a factor in the improved retention of current students, our next topic.

RETENTION

The recruitment and retention of students are intimately intertwined. The more a college is able to retain its current students, the fewer students it needs to recruit to maintain a stable enrollment. On the other hand, the seeds of the retention of current students are sown in an admissions program.

Beyond some of the admissions programs already mentioned that have improved student–institution match, undoubtedly the increased number of applications for admission has also been a factor in DePauw's improved retention. Given its commitment to maintaining its current enrollment size, an increased number of applications means DePauw has become more selective. This trend means each entering class in comprised of more very able students and fewer less able students. And if you have more academically self-disciplined and motivated students who also feel well matched with a university, inevitably retention increases.

Another dynamic in DePauw's admissions situation makes a contribution to retention. DePauw is a family school. In a typical entering class, 10 to 12 percent of the entering students will have a mother or father (or both) who attended DePauw. About 16 to 18 percent of the class will have at least one member of the immediate family (mother, father, sister, or brother) who has attended or currently is attending DePauw. And when you expand the criterion to allow for any family tie to the university, however distant it might be, about one out of every four entering students will have some relative who has attended or currently is attending DePauw.

Undoubtedly these family ties to DePauw's loyal alumni are a factor in why DePauw has an above average return on its offers of admissions, as well as its above average retention rate. It stands to reason that students who have relatives who have attended a college will be that much more apt to know about it and to make an informed decision about its appropriateness or inappropriateness for themselves.

Another important factor in DePauw's admissions and retention stories is the university's financial aid program. As a costly, private institution it is important to have a strong financial aid program so the cost will not deter any good student from considering the university. But the quality of a student's financial aid package (the relative amounts of scholarship or grant assistance, job, and loan funds) is not only a consideration in a student's decision to apply or enroll, it also is a factor when it comes to student attrition, i.e., attrition is apt to increase as the amount of loan funds increases.

Like many places, for several years during the late 1970s and early 1980s DePauw was forced to increase the amount of loans students and families were asked to assume to support the cost of a DePauw education. In recent years, particularly the last two as a result of the sesquicentennial campaign, DePauw has been able to improve the quality of its financial aid packages, despite shrinkage in the assistance DePauw students and the university is receiving from federal and state sources. For admitted students who demonstrate financial need, loan amounts are reduced somewhat by comparison to two years ago; thus loans comprise a smaller percentage of a typical student's package.

Along with these general improvements, the university made a conscious commitment to improve considerably the scholarship or grant assistance offered to DePauw's best admitted students. Not surprisingly, the yield increased among students who were admitted and offered need-based assistance, but improved financial aid awards also may have been a factor in our increased ability to retain students.

In financial terms, DePauw's future is bright. For each of several years in the foreseeable future, new endowments for scholarship assistance are likely as a result of the sesquicentennial campaign. Particularly when compared to the financial situations of most other colleges and universities, increasingly DePauw's advantage should attract applicants, enroll admitted students, and retain students once they are on campus.

In addition to the admissions, fund-raising, academic, and co-curricular programs, which seem to have made a difference in attracting and retaining students, DePauw took some specific steps over the years aimed at students who were identified as possible dropouts. Again, these activities did not develop out of a comprehensive enrollment management plan per se. Initially discussions about attrition and retention issues arose in the provost's staff meetings, principally with the dean of students, the registrar, and the director of admissions. This led to the formation of a campus retention committee, chaired by the registrar. In turn, the committee's discussions led to several activities that have improved information about retention and subsequent efforts to deal with attrition.

One of the first steps taken was an improved exit interview process. Although obviously an exit interview does not have an impact on retaining the student involved, it has been crucial in learning why students are leaving DePauw. The interest shown in departing students and their reasons for leaving also may be one of the reasons why a surprising percentage of them eventually return to DePauw. Individual student statements and aggregate data have led to steps to improve retention procedures and programs.

A variety of early warning retention procedures were introduced. Mid-semester grades were sent home for freshmen and for those students on academic warning of any kind. The dean of students' staff did extensive follow-up with students who were having some kind of academic difficulty. Much of this effort has been directly related to discussions in, and decisions made by, DePauw's Scholastic Standing Committee, the faculty committee responsible for academic eligibility.

In the last half-dozen years the Scholastic Standing Committee has made general academic expectations much more clear and set them much earlier in a student's academic career. The committee believes it has communicated more effectively to students that the academic enterprise is for them, and ought to be for the students, the primary consideration.

DePauw's course registration process is another example. Each semester students preregister for classes for the following semester. When a student does not preregister for the next semester, the registrar's office immediately is in contact with the student's academic adviser to find out if there is a reason why the student has not preregistered. If it is a reason that can be addressed, action is taken right away.

Another early warning signal concerns transcript requests. If a student initiates a request for an academic transcript from the registrar's office or a financial aid transcript from the financial aid office for transfer purpose, the dean of students' office is notified. In fact, it is worth noting at this point that the dean of students' office has become the central information point for DePauw's networking system.

For years now faculty have been encouraged to call or write the dean of students' office when a student has not been in class for any extended period of time or when they have some other concern about a student. This process also continually reinforces the faculty's role in the whole retention process. Regularly, faculty make these referrals, and their interest and concern are reinforced by the activities that occur with the students involved.

Support systems also have been improved. For example, the college has expanded its commitment to counseling services on campus. More professional staff devote time to personal counseling, and a peer counseling program has been instituted. While DePauw always has had resident assistants (carefully selected upperclass students who live and work with other current students) in its residence halls, the peer counseling program encompasses all of DePauw's living units, including its extensive fraternity and sorority system. This has added one more dimension to an increasingly extensive network of support systems.

Another important development concerns the career planning and placement program. Three years ago this effort consisted of what one member of the dean of students' staff could do on a part-time basis. Now there is a good, very visible program with two full-time career counseling and placement professionals, two support staff, and a host of alumni, faculty, and staff who are participating in various career planning and placement activities. For all students, but particularly for those who are undecided or floundering in some way when it comes to academic and career goals, this center has become an important addition and dimension to the retention of students.

Undoubtedly the writing, quantitative reasoning, and self-expression centers established in the last few years also have made a contribution to DePauw's increased retention. So have the improvements made in the quality of living facilities and the living options available to our students. A significant amount of planning time currently is focused on how the university can encourage and create new dimensions to living and learning options, all of which should subtly reinforce retention efforts.

Although DePauw's admissions and academic programs are factors, the trend in DePauw's retention also has been a significant factor in the improvement of the quality of the student body. Table 7.1 shows retention figures for the last eight years. Figure 7.1 provides a further breakdown between expected losses of students (factors essentially beyond DePauw's control) and unexpected losses (those over which presumably DePauw might have some control). Again, the trend is very noticeable.

But there is a bottom line to all that has been accomplished in the last decade. It really comes down to individual people who have had the freedom to implement their ideas. In some cases new financial resources have been important, but with most of the ideas and programs that have been implemented, they are the result of people who had the vision and perseverance to see their ideas through. DePauw no longer has a provost position, and the director of admissions and the dean of students now report to the executive vice president, not the academic vice president. The retention committee has not felt the need to meet in a few years, but the registrar, the dean of students, and the director of admissions continue to meet every 2 to 3 weeks to compare notes, inevitably dealing from time to time with attrition and retention issues.

THE FUTURE

Generally, DePauw's future looks very bright. DePauw's selectivity in admissions has increased considerably. In turn, academic standards have

Table 7.1 Retention of New Freshmen, 1977–84

Year Entered	Percentage Enrolled 1 Year Later	Percentage Enrolled 2 Years Later	Percentage Enrolled 3 Years Later	Percentage Graduated in 4 Years
1977	83.5	71.2	67.0	59.5
1978	85.1	75.0	70.2	63.8
1979	89.0	75.9	71.2	65.7
1980	85.8	74.7	71.7	66.9
1981	88.0	79.9	75.0	70.0
1982	89.5	79.9	76.2	
1983	90.6	83.1		
1984	91.4			

been raised and faculty continue to be interested in improving the academic and intellectual life of the campus. On top of that the physical plant is updated and ready for the decades ahead, and certainly several million dollars of new endowment each year will provide financial stability and the resources for future innovation. But there have been a couple of developments during the last two years that bear watching, especially in terms of DePauw's management of its enrollment.

The first began in the spring of 1984 when DePauw retained a nationally recognized, outside consultant to take a comprehensive look at the university, asking him to make specific recommendations about ways DePauw could improve itself even more.

One recommendation was that DePauw establish a long-range planning group and process. Therefore, in September 1984, DePauw's University Priorities Committee (UPC) was formed. Composed of DePauw's three vice presidents, the director of admissions, and 8 to 10 faculty at any given time, UPC is charged with making specific recommendations about De-Pauw's future to the president of the university.

The committee's first step was to develop a statement that would outline what it felt were DePauw's historic strengths and mission, that is, the philosophical underpinnings for DePauw's future. Although only a series of statements about the committee's feelings, the document guides the committee in making its recommendations. UPC's mission statement, as with all of its recommendations, was made public to everyone in the DePauw community. (It was never intended to be a public relations document outside the university, only an internal, working document.)

The Priorities committee took its mission statement to a retreat with the board of trustees in October 1984. Committee members discussed the document and long-range planning in detail with the trustees, but there

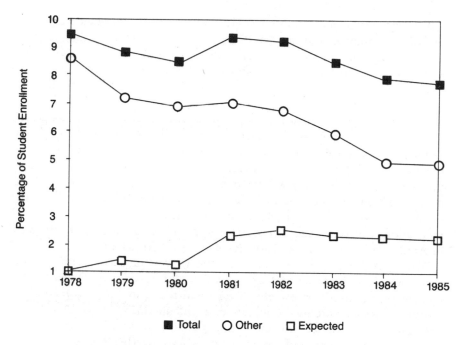

■ Total   ○ Other   □ Expected

*Expected losses include the following categories: completed residence requirements; completing requirements in evening division; special student or auditor; health/death.

Figure 7.1. Student Loss Over the Summer, 1978–85.

was one sentence from the entire four-page document that was singled out for priority consideration: "DePauw should become a more selective university."

For the balance of 1984–85 UPC considered that sentence and the ways to accomplish it. Although obviously the university's admissions and financial aid programs had become increasingly successful, the committee spent nearly all its time investigating ways that end could be furthered even more.

The recommendations and adjustments made were many and varied. To cite a few examples, the admissions application was improved to be more congruent, in look and in content, with that of other selective colleges. Funds from new scholarship endowments were earmarked to improve the academic scholarships and financial aid packages of DePauw's best admitted students. Summer academic programs for high school students were expanded and, in general, ways in which the academic and intellectual life of the campus could be improved were examined closely.

The committee met almost weekly for the entire academic year. The Priorities committee did not make any of its work secret, inviting general campus comment on its recommendations at every turn, but recommendations that might have taken years to wind through the university's governance system in the past were now made relatively quickly and directly to the president.

The 1985–86 year has brought an intense, year-long look at the academic and intellectual life of the campus. The possible expansion of DePauw's faculty, faculty development, and the general living and learning environment of the campus have come under close scrutiny. The primary assumption has been that if DePauw is to attract increased numbers of the nation's most able students and potential leaders, its academic program and quality of life will be primary considerations for those students. UPC's recommendations this year, recommendations to be made to the board of trustees in April 1986, should make DePauw even more attractive.

The second major development that bears watching, and certainly one that will have a significant impact on DePauw's future, is the January 1986 announcement by the president that he will retire in 1987 at the end of DePauw's sesquicentennial celebration. Simultaneously, the academic vice president has announced his intention to return to the classroom, so that DePauw is on the verge of naming its new academic leadership. Who will fill these important positions? How much vision and what particular vision will each possess? To what extent will DePauw's mission and program change?

For now, the University Priorities Committee continues its work and recommendations. The faculty, the dean of students' office, and others are looking at the general campus atmosphere and ways to improve it. Expansion of the faculty and increased funds for faculty development are likely. The admissions and financial aid offices are using expanded research information such as the College Board's Enrollment Planning Service to segment DePauw's markets and be more articulate about DePauw and its vision of itself where prospective students and their parents are concerned. Pricing strategy for the years ahead is yet another topic under consideration. But all of this probably will be, in large part, affected and directed by the two people who soon will provide DePauw's next generation of leadership.

Commentary by Don Hossler

In many ways the DePauw case study presents a sharp contrast to the other case studies discussed. The first few pages of this chapter might well elicit a response such as, "It is no wonder DePauw is doing so well, look at its resources and stability." Another plausible response to the opening pages of this chapter could be, "DePauw is in such a strong position, it does not need to be concerned about enrollments." As David Murray continues to describe what has happened at DePauw during his tenure there, however, it becomes evident that the institution has used several enrollment management concepts not only to maintain its student enrollments, but to strengthen its position among potential students. This case study helps to illustrate that enrollment management activities can be used to help institutions exert more influence over the characteristics of the students it enrolls as well as the number.

The DePauw case study is illustrative of an accrual model of change. There has never been a master plan for implementing an enrollment management system at DePauw. In fact, as David Murray notes, the term "enrollment management" is rarely used on the campus. The changes that have taken place at DePauw have evolved over time. The development of a student data base and a management information system not only enabled the institution to communicate more effectively with prospective students, but perhaps even more important, it enabled the admissions office to ask increasingly sophisticated questions about its applicant pool. Over time this has led to more effective targeting of DePauw's marketing and recruitment activities and eventually to the creation of a position devoted exclusively to enrollment-related issues.

The evolution of campus retention efforts also reflects the accrual nature of the change process at DePauw. It provides an example of how the concept of coupling can explain the organizational dimensions of an enrollment management system. Although the academic dean asked the registrar to bring together a committee to study student attrition, no specific approach or program was suggested. Over the years, the informal meetings between the registrar, the dean of students, and the director of admissions have led to the creation of several retention programs. The resulting programs that have been created or at least influenced by these informal meetings have produced changes in the institution and have broadened the institutional focus on enrollments beyond simply attracting more new students. These meetings have more tightly coupled issues and administrative offices, which can have an effect on student persistence that might otherwise have gone unaddressed in any systematic fashion. As the accrual model suggests, in stable environments where there is no major impetus for change, evolutionary change and less formal coupling may be the most effective means for bringing about change.

The enrollment management model that seems to best describe the activities at DePauw is the enrollment management coordinator model.

David Murray does not serve as a centralized head of all enrollment management activities, but he does help to facilitate most of the enrollment management-related activities at DePauw. He directs the activities of the admissions and financial aid office, works closely with the dean of students, is a member of the president's administrative team, and is a member of the institutional long-range planning team. This enables him to address enrollment-related issues in a wide variety of settings, thus helping to focus and to direct the enrollment-related activities of the campus.

The description of enrollment management-related activities at DePauw also highlights the comprehensive nature of the enrollment management concept. Their studies of student choice demonstrate how such efforts can be used to increase the effectiveness of marketing and recruitment activities. Beginning with the admissions process, DePauw intentionally focuses on student–institution fit. The university makes a conscious attempt to help students determine whether or not DePauw will be the "right" kind of institution for them. This emphasis on fit appears to be positively associated with student persistence. Though such causal links are difficult to establish, retention figures suggest that the institution has been increasingly effective in identifying students who are likely to find DePauw a satisfying environment.

With its success in attracting qualified students, it might be easy for an institution such as DePauw to show little concern for student persistence. This, however, is not the case. Retention programs are difficult (but not impossible) to evaluate, but the informal meetings of the dean of students, the registrar, and the director of admissions have produced a comprehensive retention program. Faculty play an important part in retention efforts. At DePauw it appears that, through activities such as a referral system and the Scholastic Standing Committee, the faculty are involved in institutional retention efforts.

As this case study reports, DePauw is also devoting attention to its financial aid packaging policies and is beginning to look at research questions related to price thresholds for its various market segments. This is also an important element of a comprehensive enrollment management plan. These efforts, along with the college choice research that is being conducted at DePauw, indicate the usefulness of management science as part of an enrollment management system. Educational research is moving into a period in which researchers are becoming more aware that not all questions can be answered through quantitative analysis. This has called into question the value of management science approaches. Although studies of price threshold and student college choice may not enable us to accurately predict enrollment behaviors for all students, such information can help campus administrators to frame more sophisticated questions and more accurately target enrollment-related activities.

Finally, DePauw's interest in student outcomes should not be over-looked. This interest manifests itself in a number of ways. The increased emphasis on career planning and placement support indicates that the institution recognizes the importance that current students place on the ability to obtain good jobs after graduation. This can help to attract and retain students. DePauw's interest in outcomes is also reflected in its efforts to monitor student proficiency across a number of skill areas. An emphasis on skill development and assessment creates a self-correcting system. If students are not performing well, changes can be made in the curriculum; if they are performing well, this can be documented and then be included in the marketing efforts of the institution. Prospective students are at-tracted to institutions that they perceive to be of high quality.

DePauw University is in a position of strength in terms of its ability to attract students in a competitive student market. Common sense might suggest that such an institution would have little need to engage in system-atic enrollment management activities. This is not the case, however. In fact, DePauw is using enrollment management concepts to improve its market position.

The DePauw approach is not a tightly coupled, formal enrollment man-agement plan. It is not even referred to as an enrollment management system. In the first chapter of this book, it was noted that although the term enrollment management was increasingly being used, it was not nec-essarily a new concept. This case study is a good example of this point. The DePauw system has evolved; some of the steps have been planned and intentional; others have simply emerged, proved to be successful, and were then formalized and adopted by the institution. DePauw University provides a good example of a working, comprehensive enrollment man-agement system.

Chapter 8

Making the System Work

DEVELOPING ENROLLMENT MANAGEMENT SYSTEMS

The four case studies illustrate the variety of organizational and programmatic emphases that can be part of an enrollment management system. Each case study has some similarities from which generalizations can be made, but each system also has its own unique qualities. Any generalizations, however, must be made with caution. The case studies were written by an administrator who played an important role in the creation of the enrollment management system on his or her respective campus. This may have made it difficult to be totally objective about the events that took place. There may have been a tendency to put a positive interpretation on what happened. In addition, these colleges and universities represent only a small proportion of the institutions that have implemented or are developing systems. Nevertheless, these institutions were selected because of their exemplary programs and much can be learned from a careful analysis of what they are doing.

In all four cases, concerns about student enrollments were a catalyst in the development of the system. The degree of concern differed across the institutions. At DePaul University there was great anxiety about rapidly declining enrollments. At the University of Wisconsin at Oshkosh there were moderate levels of concern about declining enrollments and increasingly less capable students. The enrollments decline at Johnson County Community College was slight, but it was enough to cause the president to look at enrollment-related activities in a more systematic fashion. At DePauw University, there was a slight decline in enrollments, but the motivation for becoming more intentional about enrollment efforts seems to have come as much from the declining ability levels of new students as from falling enrollments. Based on these examples, however, it appears that apprehension over student enrollments is more likely to induce the creation of enrollment management systems.

As was posited in Chapter 3, the perceived intensity of a problem affects the rapidity and the scope of change within an organization. Generally among these four institutions, as the magnitude of the enrollment problems grew, the faster institutional change took place. Great concern over enrollments produced transformational change; lesser degrees of concern, along with other institutional variables, resulted in planned change and accrual change processes. In addition, more formal and centralized enrollment management systems were likely to emerge in settings where enrollment declines were more severe. DePaul University changed the most rapidly and has developed the most tightly coupled system. DePauw University experienced the most moderate enrollment problems among the four institutions and its model is the least centralized and evolved gradually.

The rate and scope of the change should not be totally attributed to the nature of the enrollment problems. DePauw is a small, selective, liberal arts college; typically such campuses have a tradition of collegiality that makes change slow because everyone participates. Johnson County Community College, on the other hand, was able to bring about organizational restructuring quickly. This may have been the result of governance norms that exist at most community colleges. At most community colleges the decision-making process is more centralized, thus making it easier for the president and other administrators to implement organizational change.

In three of the case studies a senior administrative officer appears to have had an important facilitative role in the creation of a system. At Johnson County Community College and the University of Wisconsin at Oshkosh, support and other initiatives from the president established an environment that encouraged the development of enrollment management systems. At DePaul University, the academic vice president seems to have played this catalytic role. Because of the loosely coupled and evolutionary nature of the DePauw system, it is more difficult to determine if a senior administrator played a critical role in the development of its system.

On all four campuses there were "idea champions" that advanced the programmatic ideas that have become their enrollment management systems. At Johnson County it was Will Chatham, the Director of Admissions, Records, and Financial Aid, who played this role. At Oshkosh, it was Tom Snider, who was initially the Director of Admissions, who worked with other administrators to create the system that is now in place. At DePaul the "idea champion" was Patricia Ewers, the Academic Vice President, who played the role of key enabler as well as that of program initiator. At DePauw, there appear to have been several important program initiators including the director of admissions, the dean for student affairs, and the registrar. Generally, these were not chief administrative officers but middle managers who had earned respect among their colleagues.

In each setting, the campuses were willing to take some risks. Peters and Waterman (1982) note that one attribute of effective companies is that they are risk-taking rather than risk-aversive organizations. Patricia Ewers frankly discusses some of the costs borne by DePaul as it created its system. The University of Wisconsin at Oshkosh actually raised admission standards in the midst of campus-wide concerns about declining enrollments. DePauw University reduced the number of high school visits it was making while at the same time attempting to increase its enrollments. Most colleges and universities do just the opposite when they are hoping to attract more students.

Other similarities among the case studies include an important role for the faculty and an increased reliance on information to direct enrollment management efforts. At Johnson County Community College and the University of Wisconsin at Oshkosh, the faculty are identified as the key element in student retention efforts. At DePaul each individual college has developed its own enrollment goals and is working with the enrollment management division to create programs that meet its own specific needs. David Murray states that the emphasis on program quality and a renewed emphasis on learning outcomes have been key elements in DePauw's success in attracting high ability students. Effective enrollment management efforts require faculty support and involvement.

Research and evaluation are essential ingredients of the systems at all four institutions. Marketing information has enabled Oshkosh to develop new policies and programs that have altered the image of the campus. Research efforts have identified potential dropouts and proactive retention programs are in place to serve these students. Even academic course planning and textbook orders are keyed to the student enrollment information system developed at Oshkosh. Johnson County is using market information from potential students as well as their parents to develop marketing activities and academic program planning. DePaul is developing some sophisticated enrollment projection tools to target its recruitment efforts. DePauw has been conducting some exemplary market overlap studies in order to determine who they compete with for students and how they can be more effective in attracting the students they want. The research process is not a static one at any of these institutions. There is no "data paralysis" that delays policy making until all the results are in. Instead, research on these campuses is an iterative process, where each round of questions and answers leads to new questions. At any time new information may lead to the conclusion that the previous set of answers and subsequent decisions should be reconsidered.

Finally, one additional parallel activity found at all four institutions is the integration of enrollment management concerns and strategies into the strategic planning process. Muston (1984) found this to be an important attribute of successful enrollment management efforts. At DePaul University, Patricia Ewers is a member of the senior administrative planning team. Enrollment issues are an important part of the campus-wide planning process at Oshkosh. David Murray is a member of the planning committee at DePauw. Enrollment planning has been more directly linked to academic planning at Johnson County Community College. All four case studies discuss how enrollment-related issues have been included in the ongoing planning process at each institution.

Despite the many similarities, there are also differences in the systems created at each of the colleges and universities. A comprehensive enrollment management system includes all aspects of the student experience. In all four case studies there is a heavy emphasis on marketing, admissions, and recruitment. The enrollment management systems at DePauw University and the University of Wisconsin at Oshkosh included a strong retention program component. Although both Johnson County Community College and DePaul University address the importance of retention, very little has been accomplished. Monitoring the campus environment to enhance student–institution fit is also part of a comprehensive system, but the case studies suggest that few programmatic thrusts are being made in this area. The importance DePauw attaches to campus visits and the institutional desire to make sure that students will find the institution a good match represents some effort to enhance fit, but generally all four enrollment management systems are lacking in this area.

Attention to student outcomes is also uneven among the four colleges and universities. DePauw describes the development of upper class seminars and a thorough assessment of the outcomes of the undergraduate curriculum, both of which arose out of a concern for the cognitive outcomes of attending the university. Johnson County Community College surveyed both alumni and employers to assess the degree to which the college is preparing people for careers. It appears, however, that little attention is being given to assessing student outcomes at DePaul or Oshkosh. The ability to demonstrate that students are learning and growing can have a positive impact on enrollments. This has been the experience at Northwestern Missouri State University and Alverno College.

An analysis of the four enrollment management systems suggests that older and more established programs include a wider range of enrollment-related issues. Newly established systems, not surprisingly, tend to first focus on the areas of greatest concern. It is encouraging to note that the more established systems at Oshkosh and DePauw are effectively addressing issues such as student retention and student outcomes.

The case studies included in this volume range from relatively new enrollment management systems that are just emerging to established programs. Some systems evolved rapidly because of administrative leadership and external environmental pressures. On some campuses, tightly coupled, centralized systems have been created; at others the system is more informal and loosely coupled. None of the four case studies could be described as a pure example of one of the four models described in Kemerer, Baldridge, and Green (1982). Oshkosh, for example, has a centralized enrollment management division, but there is a matrix arrangement among the offices of admissions, financial aid, athletics, and minority and multicultural affairs. At the other extreme, DePauw University's structure is not even called enrollment management and is so informally structured that it does not seem to fit any of the archetypal models. The point of this is to reiterate that there is not one best model. Each campus needs to find the system that is most appropriate.

STAFFING THE SYSTEM

The most frequent question raised by aspiring enrollment managers is, How can I develop an enrollment management system? The implicit focus of this question seems to be, How can I create the necessary organizational structure? Questions of organizational structure are important; without them it will be difficult for viable enrollment management systems to function. Staffing, however, may be even more important. Without a knowledgeable and well-trained staff the system will not function, even with a well thought out organizational structure. My sense is that administrators, who are trained to think in terms of span of control and organizational hierarchy, are overly concerned about structure and give insufficient attention to substantive questions related to staff skills and expertise.

Staff roles in enrollment management systems need to be reconceptualized at almost every level. In addition to good management and interpersonal skills, other competencies are necessary for all administrators who are part of the system. Admissions officers should no longer describe their roles by their geographical territories. Instead, admissions offices need in-house experts in nonprofit marketing, college choice research, management information systems, and financial aid. Financial aid offices likewise need not only administrators for the GSL programs and the Pell Grants, but data base systems personnel, in-house researchers, and liaisons with admissions. As Graff (1986a) notes, registrars do not just keep transcripts; they are often the focal point in the creation of a student data base.

Orientation directors need to have a background in socialization theories and be familiar with various assessment instruments that can enhance student advising and course placement. Other student life administrators need to be skilled at environmental assessment and campus ecology intervention techniques. Colleges and universities should appoint retention officers who are familiar with the retention literature, who can work effectively with faculty and other administrators across functional areas, and who have some background in research and evaluation. The enrollment management system must have access to the institutional research office and have a high priority in the work load. In addition, there must be an institutional commitment to student outcomes research.

Despite the increased interest in the concept of enrollment management, the term has come to be equated with the functions of the admissions office. A review of many of the position announcements in the *Chronicle of Higher Education,* which use terms like enrollment management or enrollment planning, supports this conclusion. A comprehensive system goes beyond the elements of an admissions management system. An enrollment management system is a complex and elusive concept that is comprised of people and the organizational structure. Successful systems cut across traditional functional lines and are more concerned with effectiveness than boundaries of administrative units. Academic programs influence student college choice so that enrollments are not just the concern of the admissions office. On-campus jobs increase the persistence rates of students who work in those jobs. This makes it important for the retention officer, the career planning and placement office, and the financial aid office to work together to encourage as many students as possible to work on campus. Successful enrollment management systems are characterized by fluid organizational boundaries and heterarchy rather than hierarchy and span of control. The following conditions will facilitate the development of an effective system:

1. Senior level administrators interested and supportive of the concept
2. The presence of key staff members in the areas of admissions, registration and records, financial aid, retention, and other student affairs areas, or the freedom to hire new staff members if necessary
3. The presence of an institutional research office, and access to it; or if one is not present, the resources to create an in-house research unit
4. A computerized tracking and management information system and the necessary staff to use it effectively. If the support system is not there, resources to develop one and train a staff to use it appropriately
5. An organizational environment that encourages risk taking and is more concerned with effectiveness than with individual turf and bureaucratic policies

ENROLLMENT MANAGERS

The most important people in the system and perhaps the most difficult to find are individuals who will take the leadership roles in coordinating or directing an enrollment management system. An enrollment manager should have strong administrative skills and be able to command the respect of the faculty. Familiarity with the principles of marketing, student college choice, and student–institution fit and student attrition are required. In addition, enrollment managers must have a research orientation, not necessarily the competence to do the research, but certainly the ability to ask the right questions and to have some understanding of the answers to those questions. Finally, they need to have some experience with computers and related technology. This is an emerging administrative area and this combination of skills and knowledge is not easily found. Many individual campuses may find it more expedient in the long run to "grow their own" enrollment management team. In some cases admissions officers, registrars, and financial aid officers may have the necessary background, but their training and experiences do not always prepare them to take on a broader campus view or provide a research orientation. Student affairs officers with a research background and an understanding of the admissions and financial aid arenas can make viable candidates. Faculty in the social sciences with some administrative background may also be potential enrollment managers.

The downward pressures of demographic trends as well as public policy issues on student enrollments will continue to affect many institutions until the end of this century. For some institutions, the struggle to maintain viable levels of enrollments will persist. The factors that affect student enrollments at individual colleges and universities are complex. Careful analysis and planning are required to enable institutions to influence these factors. This is the task of an enrollment management system.

Bibliography

Astin, A. W. 1976. *Preventing students from dropping out.* San Francisco: Jossey-Bass.

Astin, A. W. 1985. *Achieving educational excellence.* San Francisco: Jossey-Bass.

Backoff, R. W. and Mitnick, B. M. 1981. The systems approach, incentive relations, and university management. In J. A. Wilson (ed.), *New directions in higher education: Management science applications to academic administration.* San Francisco: Jossey-Bass.

Baldridge, J. V. 1983. Organizational characteristics of colleges and universities. In J. V. Baldridge and T. E. Deal (eds.), *The dynamics of organizational change in education.* Berkeley, Calif.: McCutchan.

Bean, J. P. 1980. Dropouts and turnover: The synthesis and test of a causal model of student attrition. *Research in Higher Education* 12:155–182.

Bean, J. P. 1983. The application of a model of job turnover in work organizations to the student attrition process. *Review of Higher Education* 6:129–148.

Bean, J. P. 1986. Assessing and reducing attrition. In D. Hossler (ed.), *New directions in higher education: Managing college enrollments.* San Francisco: Jossey-Bass.

Boyer, C. M. 1986. Personal communication.

Boyer, C. M. and McGuinness, A.C. 1986. State initiatives to improve undergraduate education: ECS Survey Highlights. *AAHE Bulletin, 3:3–9.*

Cartter, A. 1966. The supply and demand for college teachers. *Journal of Human Resources* 1:22–38.

Chronicle of Higher Education, 1982. 25(13):1, 7.

———. 1983. 27(9):1, 14–15.

———. 1984. 29(16):1, 14.

———. 1985. 30(23):1, 18.

———. 1985. 30(23):1, 15.

———. 1985. 31(9):1, 18.

———. 1986. 31(18):1, 9.

Cohen, M. D. and March, J. D. 1974. *Leadership and ambiguity: The American college presidency.* New York: McGraw-Hill.

Cope, R. and Hannah, W. 1975. *Revolving college doors: The causes and consequences of dropping out, stopping out and transferring.* New York: Wiley.

Crossland, F. 1980. Learning to cope with the downward slope. *Change Magazine* 12(5):18–25.

Cyert, R. M. 1981. Management science and university management. In J. A. Wilson (ed.), *New directions in higher education: Management science applications to academic administration.* San Francisco: Jossey-Bass.

Daft, R. L. and Becker, S. W. 1978. *The innovative organization. Innovation and adoption in school organizations.* New York: Elsevier.

El-Khawas, E. 1985. *Campus reports, 1984.* Washington, D.C.: American Council on Education.

Feldman, K. A. and Newcomb, T. M. 1969. *The impact of college on students, Vol. 1.* San Francisco: Jossey-Bass.

Frances, C. 1984. 1985: The economic outlook for higher education. *AAHE Bulletin* 37(4):3–6.

Freeman, H. B. 1984. Impact of no-need scholarships on the matriculation decisions of academically talented students. Paper presented at the annual meeting of the American Association of Higher Education, Chicago, Ill.

Fullan, M. 1982. *The meaning of educational change.* New York: Teachers College Press, Columbia University.

Gardener, R. W., et al. 1985. *Asian Americans: Growth, change, diversity.* Washington, D.C.: Population Reference Bureau, Inc.

Gillespie, D. A. and Carlson, N. 1983. *Trends in financial aid: 1963 to 1983.* New York: College Entrance Examination Board.

Graff, A. S. 1986a. Organizing the resources that can be effective. In D. Hossler (ed.), *New directions in higher education: Managing college enrollments.* San Francisco: Jossey-Bass.

———. 1986b. Mobilizing for institutional change. Paper presented at conference, Enrollment Planning: A Total Institutional Approach, sponsored by the Southern Regional Office of The College Board and the University of Southern Mississippi, New Orleans, La.

Gratz, R. D. and Salem, P. J. 1981. *Organizational communication and higher education.* AAHE-ERIC/Higher Education Research Report No. 10. Washington, D.C.: American Association for Higher Education.

Green, K. C. 1982. The transition from high school to college: Expectations and realities. Paper presented at the Midwestern Regional Assembly of the College Board, Chicago, Il, February 1982.

Haines, R. W. 1984. The debate over no-need scholarships. *Change Magazine,* 16(16):25, 28–31.

Hall, R. A. 1981. Contemporary organizational theory and higher education: A mismatch. In J. A. Wilson (ed.), *New directions for higher education: Management science applications to academic administration.* San Francisco: Jossey-Bass.

Havelock, R. G. 1973. *The change agent's guide to innovation in education.* Englewood Cliffs, N.J.: Educational Technology Publications.

Hearn, J. C. and Loganecker, D. 1985. Enrollment effects of alternative postsecondary pricing policies. *Journal of Higher Education,* 56(5):485–500.

Henckley, S. P. and Yates, J. R. 1974. *Futurism in education: Methodologies.* Berkeley, Calif.: McCutchan.

Hispanics: Challenges and opportunities. 1984. New York: The Ford Foundation.

Hodgkinson, H. L. 1983. *Guess who's coming to college: Your students in 1990.* Washington, D.C.: National Institute of Independent Colleges and Universities.

———. 1985. *All one system: Demographics of education, kindergarten through graduate school.* Washington, D.C.: Institute for Educational Leadership, Inc.

———. 1986. Guess who's coming to college in Indiana. Paper presented at Indiana University, Bloomington, Ind.

Hossler, D. 1984. *Enrollment management: An integrated approach.* New York: College Entrance Examination Board.

———. 1985. Studying college choice: A three phase model and the research agenda. Paper presented at the Second Annual Chicago Conference on Enrollment Management: An Integrated Strategy for Institutional Vitality, sponsored by the Midwestern Regional Office of The College Board and Loyola University of Chicago, Chicago, Ill.

———. 1986. *New directions in higher education: Managing college enrollments.* San Francisco: Jossey-Bass.

Huddleston, T. 1984. Effective organizational structures for enrollment management. Paper presented at First Annual Conference on Leadership for Enrollment management: An Integrated Strategy for Institutional Vitality, sponsored by the Midwestern Regional Office of The College Board and Loyola University of Chicago, Chicago, Ill.

Ihlanfeldt, W. 1980. *Achieving optimal enrollments and tuition revenues.* San Francisco: Jossey-Bass.

Iverson B. K., Pascarella, E. T. and Terenzini, P. T. 1984. Informal faculty-student contact and commuter college freshmen. *Research in Higher Education,* 21(2):123–136.

Jackson, G. 1978. Financial aid and student enrollments. *Journal of Higher Education,* 49:548–74.

———. 1982. Public efficiency and private choice in higher education. *Educational evaluation and policy analysis,* 4(2):237–247.

Jackson, R. and Chapman, R. 1984. The effects of merit-based aid on student college choice. Paper presented at the Annual Forum of The College Board, New York, N.Y.

Kemerer, F. R., Baldridge, J. V. and Green, K. C. 1982. *Strategies for effective enrollment management.* Washington D.C.: American Association of State Colleges and Universities.

Kerchner, C. T. and Schuster, J. H. 1982. The use of crisis: Taking the tide at the flood. *Review of Higher Education,* 5(3):125–42.

Kreutner, L. and Godfrey, E. S. 1981. Enrollment management: A new vehicle for institutional renewal. *The College Board Review* No. 118 (Winter 1980–81).

Kuh, G. D. 1981. *Indices of quality in the undergraduate experience.* AAHE-ERIC/ Higher Education Research Report No. 4. Washington, D.C.: American Association of Higher Education.

Lindquist, J. 1978. *Strategies for change.* Berkeley, Calif.: Pacific Soundings Press.

Lippitt, R., Watson, J., and Westley, R. 1958. *The dynamics of planned change: A comparative study of principles and techniques.* New York: Harcourt Brace.

Litten, L. H. 1986. Perspectives on pricing. In D. Hossler (ed.), *New directions in higher education: Managing college enrollments.* San Francisco: Jossey-Bass.

Litten, L. H. and Brodigan, D. 1982. Background music. *College and University,* 57(3), 242–64.

Manski, C. F. and Wise, D. A. 1983. *College choice in America.* Cambridge, Mass.: Harvard University Press.

Maguire, J. and Lay, R. 1980. Identifying the competition in higher education. *College and University,* 56:53–65.

———. 1981. Modeling the college choice process. *College and University,* 56(2):123–39.

Maguire, J. 1984. *The enrollment management lecture series.* 6 videotapes. Concord, Mass.: Enrollment Management Consultants.

Mikulecky, L. 1985. A response to the NAEP reading report card. Occasional paper, School of Education, Indiana University, Bloomington, Ind.

Miner, A. S. and Estler, S. E. 1985. Accrual mobility: Job mobility in higher education through responsibility accrual. *Journal of Higher Education,* 56(2): 121–43.

Muston, R. 1984. Enrollment strategies among selected state universities. Paper presented at the Annual Meeting of the Association for the Study of Higher Education, Chicago, Ill.

Noel, L. et al. 1985. *Increasing student retention.* San Francisco: Jossey-Bass.

Nordvall, R. C. 1982. *The process of change in higher education institutions.* ASHE/ERIC Higher Education Research Report No. 7. Washington, D.C.: Association for the Study of Higher Education.

Novak, T. and Weiss, D. 1985a. What's All This Talk about Enrollment Management? *The Admissions Strategist* No. 4. College Entrance Examination Board.

Novak, T. and Weiss, D. 1985b. Unpublished paper. College Entrance Examination Board.

O'Neil, D. M. and Sepielli, P. 1985. *Education in the United States: 1970–85.* Washington, D.C.: U.S. Department of the Census.

Pace, C. R. 1984. *Measuring the quality of the college student experience.* Los Angeles: Higher Education Research Institute, University of California at Los Angeles.

Pascarella, E. T. 1985. A program for research and policy development on student persistence at the institutional level. Paper presented at the Second Annual Chicago Conference on Enrollment Management: An Integrated Strategy for Institutional Vitality, sponsored by The Midwestern Regional Office of The College Board and Loyola University of Chicago, Chicago, Ill.

Pascarella, E. T., Duby, P., Miller, V. and Rasher, S. 1981. Pre-enrollment variables and academic performance as predictors of freshman year persistence, early withdrawal, and stop-out behavior in an urban, non-residential university. *Research in Higher Education,* 15:329–49.

Pascarella, E. T. and Terenzini, P. T. 1980. Patterns of student–faculty interaction beyond the classroom. *Journal of Higher Education,* 48:540–52.

Peters, T. and Waterman, R. 1982. *In search of excellence: Lessons from America's best run companies.* New York: Harper & Row.

Ramist, L. 1981. *College student attrition.* New York: College Entrance Examination Board.

Sarrio, T. T. 1979. Leadership and the change process: Preparing educational administrators. In R. E. Herriott and N. Gross (eds.), *The dynamics of planned educational change*. Berkeley, Calif.: McCutchan.

Summerskill, J. 1962. Dropouts from college. In N. Sanford (ed.), *The American college*. New York: Wiley.

Statistical abstracts of the United States. 1985. Washington, D.C.: U.S. Bureau of the Census.

Trends in adult student enrollments. 1985. Washington, D.C.: National Center for Educational Statistics, U.S. Department of Education.

Zucker, J. D. and Nazari-Robati, A. 1982. Tuition and the open door: A relative perspective. *Community/Junior College Quarterly*, 6:145–55.

Update. January 1986. A report from the Washington Office of the College Board.

U.S. Department of Education. 1983. *A nation at risk: A report from the commission on excellence in education*. Washington, D.C.: Department of Education.

———. 1984. *The nation responds*. Washington, D.C.: U.S. Department of Education.

———. 1985. National Center of Education Statistics data.

Weick, K. E. 1976. Educational organizations as loosely coupled systems. *Administrative Science Quarterly*, 21(1):1–19.

Willingham, W. W. 1985. *Success in college: The role of personal and academic ability*. New York: College Entrance Examination Board.